HOW DID MY FAMILY
GET IN MY OFFICE?!

Surprising Ways Your Upbringing
Impacts You At Work
And What You Can Do About It

by

Bonnie Artman Fox, MS, LMFT

TELEMACHUS PRESS

Cover designed by Telemachus Press, LLC

Edited by Chris Murray

Cover art:
Copyright © iStock/1066106682_LeszekCzerwonda
Copyright © iStock/1069231818_TARIK KIZILKAYA

Published by Telemachus Press, LLC
7652 Sawmill Road
Suite 304
Dublin, Ohio 43016
www.TelemachusPresss.com

Visit the author website: www.BonnieArtmanFox.com

ISBN: 978-1-948046-83-1 (eBook)
ISBN: 978-1-948046-84-8 (Paperback)

Library of Congress Control Number: 2020922196

Category: BUSINESS & ECONOMICS / Leadership

Version 2020.11.12

Praise For
How Did My Family Get In My Office?!

"'Leaders are made, not born' is something the author knows all too well. Leaders need to be able to lead themselves before they lead others. In this enlightening book, Bonnie tells the story of eleven leaders whose persistence and tenacity (combined into 'pertinacity') guides them on a journey to self-awareness and profound transformation of their leadership styles. Whether in the all-important domain of conflict management, a major theme of the book, or in the area of relationship building, Bonnie very engagingly shows us that our past experiences do not have to define our future. The book offers deep insights into the roots of personal leadership and the overarching chapter structure, based on a step-by-step approach, offers wonderful clarity, including exercises for self-reflection. *This is a must-read book to more fully understand leadership!*"

George Kohlrieser, Ph.D.
Distinguished Professor of Leadership and Organizational Behaviour
International Institute for Management Development, Switzerland
Bestselling Author of *Hostage at the Table* and *Care to Dare*

"Many leaders avoid conflict because it's messy and uncomfortable. Based on their family histories, the leaders in this book show us how to develop the interpersonal courage necessary for productive conflict which will ultimately result in healthier teams and more effective organizations."

Patrick Lencioni
President and CEO, The Table Group
Best-selling author of *The Five Dysfunctions of a Team*

"Leadership is all about relationship, and where did we first learn about relationship? In our families, of course, and Bonnie Artman Fox skillfully shows how family history can damage our work interactions. Fox offers the insight we need to analyze our Family Factor, as well as providing simple and effective strategies to resolve its counterproductive influence."

Laura Crawshaw, Ph.D., LCSW
Founder, The Boss Whispering Institute
Author of *Taming The Abrasive Manager: How To End Unnecessary Roughness In the Workplace*

"Bonnie Artman Fox has provided a clear view and understanding of how our family of origin affects our ability to communicate in the workplace. *How Did My Family Get In My Office?!* answers the question that I and others often ask ourselves after a stressful encounter in the workplace: 'Why did I say that, or act that way?' This thoughtful and thought-provoking book illuminates some of the reasons why we act and communicate ineffectively on the jobs. Bonnie delineates successful strategies to understand and adapt our actions and words to improve our ability to communicate effectively at work. It should be required reading in graduate schools and corporation training programs alike."

Tony Pacione, LCSW
Deputy Director, Illinois Lawyers' Assistance Program

"When working with leaders to help them address disruptive behaviors, I often find a common barrier that prevents them from doing this. That barrier is their strong desire to avoid conflict. Many of the leaders I work with admit that they hate confronting people because it makes them so uncomfortable or they address disruptive behaviors in a way that comes across as too abrasive. It's a problem that prevents leaders from setting behavioral expectations and actually holding employees accountable for professional behavior.

Then I read Bonnie's book, *How Did My Family Get In My Office?!* and it all made sense. Through the stories from leaders and how their upbringing determined whether they avoid conflict or pound conflict over the head, understanding the 'Family Factor' was so insightful! Once leaders understand the role their family plays in their current role as a leader, only then they can recognize their patterns and more importantly—change them.

I highly recommend Bonnie's book to people who find themselves in a leadership role who truly want to cultivate a strong cohesive team of professionals."

Dr. Renee Thompson
CEO & Founder, Healthy Workforce Institute
Author of *Enough! Eradicate Bullying & Incivility In Healthcare Strategies for Front Line Leaders*

"This is a truly important book. In an era when leaders must show up as the best version of themselves to be successful, this book can prompt the deep reflection and examination required to create self-aware leaders. Relatable, powerful stories coupled with Bonnie's thought-provoking expertise make this a must-read for leaders at all levels."

Joe Mull, M.Ed., CSP
Author of *No More Team Drama and Cure for the Common Leader*

"When coaching leaders and their work teams with issues like conflict, I often sense that I am missing something, that there are powerful forces existing in the shadows. In *How Did My Family Get Into My Office?!*, author Bonnie Artman Fox masterfully pulls these forces out into the light of day. As it turns out, these hidden forces are not mysterious or unknown.

They are us, our families, our upbringings. As Bonnie so clearly states, 'The Family Factor.'

How Did My Family Get In My Office?! offers compelling personal stories from eleven corporate leaders, each revealing how 'The Family Factor' has influenced their leadership style, with specific focus given to how they handle workplace conflict. Bonnie offers the reader a wealth of guidance with her professional observations, reflections, and powerful coaching questions.

If you are a leader or working with leaders, *How Did My Family Get In My Office?!* is a must. I know that a copy will be kept at my ready access."

Sam Anderson
Director, Washington EAP Services and Leadership Coach

"The stories in this book will jump off the page and illustrate ways in which your family dynamics show up in your office every day! Filled with practical ways to work through conflict with coworkers who remind you of your own family, this book shows leaders how to change the only person you can change, you."

Sara Droddy, SHRM-CP, PHR
Franciscan University of Steubenville

"As a psychotherapist, one of my specialties is helping clients manage issues in their workplace. Some of these clients come to me with little understanding of therapy, how it works, and what it can do for them.

While I know of books which show how therapy can improve people's lives and relationships, few explain the relationship between what my clients learned as children and the outcomes they experience at work.

Imagine my delight that Bonnie Artman Fox has written such a book! As a psychotherapist turned workplace conflict expert and leadership coach, Bonnie knows well the two worlds of the office and the couch. Her book, written simply and clearly, tells the stories of eleven people who (unconsciously) brought their families into their offices, and the changes they needed to make in order to shoo them out the door once again.

With such clear examples, readers don't need to know anything about therapy in order to get the full impact of this book. By reading it, they will learn that recognizing the dysfunctional patterns from their childhoods can help them to reinvent their lives in the workplace as well as at home.

I thoroughly enjoyed this book and believe it will make an excellent contribution to the field. I imagine recommending it to many future clients as an adjunct to our work in therapy."

Tory Butterworth, Ph.D.
Licensed Professional Counselor
Body-Centered Psychotherapy

"An entertaining, touching, and enlightening take on what makes leaders who they are. Bonnie presents us with a compelling variety of candid autobiographies. Using clinical and managerial research, and her own keen insight, she then shows readers how to recognize where we've come from, how to keep the good, and how to come to terms with the not-so-good. Leaders at all levels will find rich lessons and practical guidance on applying them in their own lives."

Barry Wolfe
President, Argos HR Solutions, LLC
Author of *The Little Black Book of Human Resources Management*

"In *How Did My Family Get In My Office?!* Bonnie addresses the fundamental question we must address when faced with conflict at work; what she calls The Family Factor. The book helps anyone to reflect on what we learned growing up and provides practical steps any of us can apply to deal with people more effectively as adults. The personal stories shared by leaders helps to see how our handprint might be on the crime scene."

Doug Johnston
Advisor and Facilitator
Author of *Thriving in Conflict*, Speaker

"Bonnie Artman Fox brings to life the most common struggles of conflict in the workplace that especially hit home with family-owned businesses. This book will inspire you to mend family rifts and implement the strategies provided to resolve differences with family members and co-workers alike."

Sue Reilly
Executive Director
Family Business Alliance, Wilkes University/Penn State Scranton, PA

This book is dedicated to the leaders you'll meet in the following pages who allowed me to share their stories.

Your transparency, self-awareness, and courage are an inspiration to me and will inspire many for years to come to face conflict in healthy, productive ways. Thank you.

Contents

FOREWORD

Author's note: The following Foreword was written by "June," a corporate leader in a highly competitive industry who tells her story of overcoming the impact of very difficult family circumstances in Chapter 3.

When I turned 32 I thought to myself that I never expected to still be alive. My life had been one of living with an alcoholic parent and being an alcoholic myself. There had been no five-year plan, no expectations to be successful. My focus was on when I would be having my next drink. If I were still alive at 32, I had expected to be on the same barstool in DeKalb that I occupied during my college years.

My work life reflected the chaos of my personal life. At work, I was an aggressive leader because command-and-control aggressiveness was the only type of leadership I had ever known. As you will read in my story in Chapter 3, I had no empathy for my employees because I have never received any empathy from others, and didn't see the need for it. And most of all, I endured years of abuse from a boss, that I never should have accepted. But after all, abusive behavior was what I was used to. I now know that my work behavior and decisions reflected what Bonnie Artman Fox calls in this book "The Family Factor": the experiences of my childhood were driving the choices I was making in my workplace.

As it turns out, I made it out of the house, off the barstool and became a leader in business—by the grace of God, changing my thought process with the help of great therapists.

Bonnie has been an important influence in my life. At that fateful age of 32, I happened to read an article in a magazine about adult children of alcoholics and then realized that was something I could grab on to. I called the Employee Assistance Program hotline to ask for a counselor for adult children of alcoholics and I began my journey of recovery. After a few appointments, I was able to recognize and admit that I, too, was an alcoholic. I spoke with my parents and they said they would support whatever I needed to get my act together. Many hard questions later, my mom started in Al-anon and seeing my success, she started seeing a counselor—and that would be Bonnie Artman Fox. My siblings and I met with Bonnie and my mom to help us all improve our communication skills.

I continued in personal counseling and was fortunate to work in a company that supported individual growth. I had some great mentors in the business environment as well. Through on-going therapy and corporate support classes, I grew into being a good manager and helped others achieve success personally and in business. I was able to shed the "way we were brought up" attitude that my parents used and created a new framework for my personal life and work life. Just because we were raised a certain way doesn't mean we need to continue down that path. Break the mold, try a new way. If you fail at least you tried. That is how I try to live. Yes, there are times I still fear change, but then I face the fear and try it anyway.

I am so blessed to have been on this journey. I am a better person for tackling the alcoholism and adversity that came with it. The hiding, the lying, the shame—all of that is behind me and I feel grateful every day. I bring that attitude to work with me and watch the paradigm shift around me.

Bonnie has been an advocate for us recovering folks and wrote this book in collaboration with myself and others who have made the choice to break the pattern and become leaders—in spite of our beginnings. I hope you take what you need from our stories and the lessons drawn from each story by Bonnie, and share the message. You are not alone in the way the experiences of your younger years influence your life as an adult, and as leader. You, too, can recover and break the pattern.

—June (Chapter 3)

HOW DID MY FAMILY GET IN MY OFFICE?!

Surprising Ways Your Upbringing
Impacts You At Work
And What You Can Do About It

INTRODUCTION

Conflict in the workplace is costly to organizations. According to one study, 85 percent of U.S. employees surveyed experience conflict on some level. To make matters worse, over half of employees (54 percent) believe leaders don't intervene early enough when conflict occurs. As a result, employees reported losing 2.8 hours a week because of unresolved conflict, which costs organizations $359 billion in paid hours a year. Another study, reported in *Fortune*, showed that managers and executives of Fortune 1000 firms spend 13 percent of their time at work, or the equivalent of seven weeks a year, dealing with the aftermath of incivility and mending employee relationships.

From 25-plus years as a psychiatric nurse and licensed marriage and family therapist, I've spent thousands of hours with clients, listening to story after story about dysfunctional workplaces and bosses' erratic behavior that was taking a toll on their health. From sleepless nights and stomach problems to anxiety and depression, my clients were seeking help to deal with the stress of their jobs.

> *The Family Factor refers to the connection between how conflict was handled in your upbringing and how you handle conflict today.*

What often emerged from these sessions was the recognition that the dynamics of their work environment, especially related to conflict, were similar to their family upbringing. I came to see just how tightly work life is an extension of early family life.

I call this the *Family Factor*™. The Family Factor refers to the connection between how conflict was handled in your upbringing and how you handle conflict today. Whether we realize it or not, our behaviors and tendencies in how we relate to others, especially working through conflict, were formed in our childhood.

We're often not aware of the Family Factor but it happens to all of us. Here are some examples:

- Your boss has an angry outburst that reminds you of a parent.

- At work, you're often in the "fixer" role, picking up the pieces for underperformers as you did for a family member when you were a child.

- You find yourself caught in the middle of a conflict between co-workers as you were often caught between people when your family argued.

- You lash out at people who contradict you, just as you saw your father lash out if anyone dared contradict him.

- You're told "this is the way we do things" or "because I said so," just as you were told by a parent when you challenged the status quo.

- When conversations get tense between co-workers, you find any excuse to walk away as you did in your upbringing.

Every day throughout the world, similar scenarios happen in work settings. From corporations to non-profits to faith-based institutions, our workplace habits and reactions are more connected to the experiences of our childhood than we realize.

As a result, workplaces are often filled with the lingering tension of mishandled conflict.

In one of the tribes in Papua New Guinea, this lingering tension is referred to as the *Mokita*™ meaning "the truth we know about and agree not to speak of." In our English language, the tension is referred to as "the elephant in the room."

Whatever you call it, when conflict isn't resolved, there's often a palpable strain on communication and projects stop moving forward productively. Gossip pervades, teams are divisive, and ultimately, bottom-line results suffer.

The Science Behind the Family Factor

There is science behind the Family Factor. Neuroscientists have shown that experiences that occur during one's upbringing leave imprints on a young child's neuropathways that, as adults, we lean back on during conflict, even at work. These neuropathways relate to our natural fight or flight tendencies in the face of danger.

When you perceive a threat, such as hearing an angry tone or seeing an angry facial expression, your brain responds with a surge of stress hormones that puts your fight or flight response in full gear. In an instant, you're overwhelmed with strong emotions, such as fear, that can shut down the executive functioning of the brain that brings out your best thinking. That's when you either "fight," defending yourself by saying something you might later regret, or "flee" (flight) by literally leaving to get away from the perceived threat. Another common response is to "freeze" by staying quiet, not saying anything for fear of making a tense situation worse.

Resolving the Family Factor through Self-Awareness

The good news is that through self-awareness of the influence of your upbringing on your workplace behavior and reactions, you can recognize your Family Factor and change how you deal with conflict for the better.

When my clients saw their work and family situations as similar, they became significantly more aware of how unconsciously their own issues were sometimes contributing to their work problems. And when their unresolved upbringing issues met the unresolved upbringing issues of their co-workers and boss, it became obvious everyone was reacting out of defensiveness and self-protection. No wonder the workplace was dysfunctional and my clients were experiencing physical ailments and anxiety!

Newly aware of their role in the dysfunction at work, my clients shifted their focus from getting others to change, to how *they* could change. Instead of staying stressed out and getting burned out, they dealt with their personal struggles that were getting in the way of contributing to a healthy workplace. In many cases, their work situation improved and their new way of interacting created a positive ripple effect that prompted others to be less reactive and respond in healthier ways. In other cases, as my clients grew in their self-awareness, they decided to move on, taking their personal growth and newly learned emotional intelligence skills with them to a healthier work environment.

Once you have that self-awareness, you can learn how to manage your conflict management tendencies effectively. In this book, you'll meet eleven leaders with very different family upbringings, who did just that. To protect their privacy, the leaders' names and certain professional details were changed. The leaders chose the pseudonyms.

> *An essential attribute for managing the emotional impact of your up-bringing is "pertinacity."*

The leaders in this book considered both positive and negative events from their upbringing (their Family Factor) and learned how to successfully manage conflict at work, rejecting the unproductive habits and tendencies of the past and changing how they live and lead.

An essential attribute for managing the emotional impact of your upbringing is "pertinacity"—which is a combination of persistence and tenacity and refers to the ability to stick with something no matter what. Without pertinacity, it is too easy to revert back to the habits and reactions of the past. Transforming your conflict management style is a commitment that you are making to yourself; meeting that commitment requires pertinacity.

An important note: Family is sacred ground. The intent of the leader interviews and this book is not to blame, shame, or finger-point at parents or anyone's upbringing. Rather, it is to understand the context of events that occurred and the impact of those events on the leader's conflict style. I truly believe parents do the best they can with what they know at the time, based on their own upbringing and life experiences. All of the leaders spoke with appreciation and a positive regard for their parents and family.

Other conflict management books might give you tools or techniques. In this book, you will go to the root of why you manage conflict the way you do, which is the first step to dramatically changing and improving how you handle conflict in any situation.

How to Get the Most Out of This Book

Each of the leaders' chapters is broken into the following five sections:

1. The leaders' stories, written in their words, which describe how conflict was handled in their upbringing.

2. The leaders' descriptions of how their family dynamics or Family Factors show up at work.

3. Productive Conflict Management Strategies that the leaders identified as helping them to change their conflict patterns.

4. A section called "The Family Factor," which is my summary of how the leaders changed their conflict patterns or leveraged family strengths.

5. Self-Reflection Questions for your personal growth and self-awareness.

The closing chapter outlines the action steps you can take to gain more self-awareness in changing your conflict management style. In no way is this intended to be prescriptive. These action steps are intended as a guide for new behaviors to sink in over time when your Family Factor shows up at work.

Some of you may be thinking that the stories of the leaders don't apply to you, that "it's great for the leaders in this book that they were able to change how they deal with conflict. *BUT* you don't know my story. I'll never forget how a certain family member has wronged me. Besides, my family has nothing to do with how I get along with people at work."

If this is you, you're right, I don't know your story. I would challenge you to reconsider how unresolved family dynamics have impacted you in ways you may not realize.

In reading the stories, consider how you can relate to each leader's story. While none of the stories are graphic in detail, be aware that you may be emotionally triggered by something painful from your own upbringing. Use the self-reflection questions at the end of each chapter to apply to your life, and choose a trusted friend, coach, or therapist to discuss how the stories impact you. I hope you learn from these stories, as I learned in gathering them. Every one of us has our upbringing stories—and now we can learn how to use them to make us handle conflict more productively!

References

Global Human Capital Report. *Workplace Conflict and How Businesses Can Harness It to Thrive.* Mountain View, CA: CPP, Inc., 2008.

Porath, Christine and Christine Pearson. "The Price of Incivility." *Harvard Business Review,* January–February 2013.

You can't help men permanently by doing for them what they could and should do for themselves.

—Abraham Lincoln

CHAPTER ONE

Maria's Story
You Don't Always Have To Be The Fixer

Chapter Summary: Maria rocked the boat of her family upbringing by challenging the abusive status quo. With little support from an alcoholic father and a mother with mental illness, she learned how to navigate life at a very young age. Gratefully, she had the positive influence of her grandmother, who modeled how to take a stand for her own well-being. At the same time, her tumultuous upbringing led her to become a "fixer"—someone who continuously takes responsibility for others. Her story reveals how to change the pattern of overfunctioning, inherited from the family system.

The Chaos of Alcoholism, Abuse, and Mental Illness

My father was an alcoholic and my mother suffers from mental illness. My father was abusive towards my mother physically, emotionally, and mentally. I'm the oldest of my parents' children and was five years old when my parents divorced. My father remarried shortly after the divorce and had two more children with his second wife, who was a wonderful woman. Even though my sister and I lived with my mother, we saw our father often. My father was all about family. We were together frequently with my father and his wife, which created a deep bond between my step-siblings and us.

My father was Puerto Rican and my mother Guatemalan. In the Puerto Rican culture, being masculine means to provide for your family. There's an unspoken message that "if I don't provide financially for my family or if the family fails, I'm not a man." The woman's role is to stay at home and take care of the family cooking and cleaning. It would be threatening to the man's masculinity if the woman would make more money than the husband. All of the care of the children comes from the woman; for example, men aren't diaper changers. If your wife doesn't listen to you, there's nothing wrong with hitting her to "put her in line." My father never hit my sister or me, I'm not sure why. His whole world was his kids and he adored us.

Drinking is also very much a part of the Puerto Rican culture. Men tend to have a machismo attitude thinking, "I am the man, you're not a man if you can't drink." My father's personality changed based on whether he was drinking. When he was drinking, he was like the devil in its purest form; when he wasn't, he was the most amazing person you could ever meet in your entire life. He was very kind and caring. Everybody loved him because he would do anything for anyone. He would go, at the most, five years sober, and that's when things were great in our relationship. Even though he went to Alcoholics Anonymous (AA), as a Puerto Rican man, he didn't think he needed help. He couldn't maintain sobriety. There were things that I witnessed in how physically abusive he was to my mom, and how he yelled and threatened her, that no child should ever see.

Even after my parents divorced, my dad continued to be very physically abusive to my mom. One time after he'd been drinking, he came to our house and was banging on the front door with a gun. The gun left a mark in the door; you could visibly see the imprint of the barrel in the door. Every time I came home, I saw that imprint and the reminder of that evening.

While my father was not physically abusive to my sister and me, my mom was very much a physical disciplinarian, which included spanking. I told her once,

"If they had child abuse back when I was little, they would have built a jail on top of you," and her response was always, "But you turned out okay." Part of her discipline was impacted by her bipolar illness, which contributed to her erratic moods.

Being the Fixer

I was often the caregiver for my sister and me because of Dad's drinking and Mom being mentally unable to care for us. Mom could be in her room for weeks at a time, primarily coming out to yell at us if we were making too much noise.

When I was growing up, Mom had Obsessive-Compulsive Disorder (OCD), so everything had to be kept very clean. The kind of clean where you could eat off of the floor! I did the majority of the cleaning and my sister helped as best she could since she was younger.

When I was eight, my grandfather built a stool for me to stand on because I was doing everything that needed to be done around the house—including making meals, ironing school uniforms, and making sure our homework got done—because my mother wasn't able to take care of us. By age eleven, I was writing checks. By age 14, I started my first job, and by age 19, I owned my own home. I've been an overachiever, partly because whenever there was conflict in the family, I took charge to smooth over the conflict and chaos. My sister and I joked around a lot growing up because we were always trying to make a bad situation better.

Before I graduated from high school, I experienced this thing called teenage pregnancy. My parents weren't around to provide structure and I could do whatever I wanted. At age 16, I had a little girl. I quickly realized, I've got this child to take care of, and I was still supporting my mom and sister; I was the only person in our home who was working. I stayed in school and after graduation began working full-time. I took classes at a local community college whenever I could afford it. My baby's father wasn't in the picture very much, but his parents are wonderful people and were very involved and helpful so that

I could stay in college. I couldn't have done all that I did without their support because I couldn't depend on my parents for help.

My father's second wife was also Guatemalan like my mother, and she was only ten years older than me. She's the nicest person you could ever imagine. My father was even more abusive to her than he was to my mother. Because she came directly from Guatemala and didn't know anyone here, I took on a motherly role with her, too, because she didn't know anything. For example, she'd never seen an escalator or been in an elevator; she didn't know any of these things we take for granted, so I taught her.

When I was around 22 or 23, I and a woman she worked with gave my father's second wife money to leave my father because of how abusive he was to her. I gave her every single penny I had. My father never forgave me for that and always brought it up to me, even just before he died. I said, "Dad, you should probably thank me. Otherwise, you might be in jail." Dad was never able to take ownership of his behavior.

My Positive Role Models

Growing up, I was always taking care of others. I had little support, with two very important exceptions: The Catholic nuns and my maternal grandmother.

I went to a Catholic school throughout my childhood. The nuns were the only ones I could talk to. They were my only sense of normal. Even though I never told them what was happening at home, they were very nice and supportive of me. When I was in grade school, I thought I wanted to be a nun when I grew up.

My primary role model, however, was and is my maternal grandmother. She has been the driving force behind my determination throughout my life. She always told me, "Anything you want to do, even if you want to cut lawns for the rest of your life, you do that. But you're going to go to college first."

Part of the reason I admire her so much is because she left my grandfather, who was abusive to her. If she hadn't taken a stand for how she was being treated and to protect her children, we wouldn't be here today.

She's the one who pushed me to be my best because there was no one else to push me. She would buy my books for school, purchase parking passes—whatever she could do to make it easier for me, she did. When I was around six, my mother went into an institution for several months, and I lived with my grandmother during that time. We have a wonderful relationship, and I still look to her for advice. I thank God for her.

My Husband's Influence

When I met my husband, he became a calming influence in my life. At one point, he questioned me: "Why are you always yelling?" I was so used to being in charge, taking care of people, I didn't realize how much I was yelling. He helped me to grow as a person and has been the first example of a positive, loving man I knew. He's always been very supportive and in his eyes there's nothing I can't do.

My husband is Mexican, and it's not uncommon as a cultural norm for Mexican men to hit their wives. In my husband's family, there was never any violence, abuse, or chaos as there was in mine. Unlike my father, who had many girlfriends while he was married, my in-laws have tremendous love and respect for one another.

How My Family Shows Up in My Office

My upbringing has had a major impact on my work, beginning with the profession that I chose. After having my daughter, I decided I wasn't going to be a nun anymore. I wanted to give back and help families affected by abuse and alcoholism similar to my upbringing. I made a conscious choice for my life never to be chaotic again or for my kids to never experience what I went through.

I got my master's degree in social work and began as a service coordinator at the same Domestic Violence agency where today I'm the CEO. I'm in the position of empowering women to get out of abusive relationships.

We work with families that are in crisis. As a leader, I make sure we meet as a team at least weekly. I know how stressful our work can be and I check in with my employees to ensure we're all doing okay. If there's something that we can do to support each other then we do that. I know what it's like to be under constant conflict and chaos and I don't want to put my employees in that situation. I want to be as supportive as I can to my staff.

My cultural background also influences my actions and skills in my workplace. As I mentioned earlier, my mom was Guatemalan and my dad was Puerto Rican. I was born in the United States, growing up in an all-white neighborhood until I was 15 years old. Navigating the Latino and white worlds growing up has also helped me navigate those two worlds in my work, because everyone I work with in our offices is Latino, including our clients. When I'm talking to funders and representing our agency in other ways outside the office, I'm definitely not in the Latino world anymore. I'm in the American culture and I have to conform to American norms.

When I was a child, we never spoke Spanish at home; it was always English. I didn't start speaking Spanish until I was an adult. When I met my husband he didn't speak English. I started really practicing my Spanish so I could talk with him! I'm not American enough to be American, but I'm also not Latino enough to be Latino because I was born in the U.S. My Spanish isn't perfect. But I use my strengths in both of these arenas to help me navigate both worlds.

Making Things Happen

My family upbringing, which included taking care of my mother and younger sister, taught me how to be a survivor and make things happen for us. I learned how to be very careful and creative in how to stay safe when either my father was in a drunken rage or my mother wasn't able to care for us. I use those same skills today in helping women and children get out of domestic violence and start a life for themselves and their children.

My role as fixer in my family taught me to be an overcomer and do what I needed to do in order to make things happen. At times, I needed to be assertive when it came to getting things for my family. In my role as CEO, there are times I need to be assertive for fundraising. Just like in my family, I move things forward. I help people get the resources they need as I did for my mother, sister, and stepmother. I care so much about the work, which stems from my life experience in my family upbringing and knowing there is a way out of abuse.

Learning to Remove Myself From the Fixer Role

In some situations, regardless of what we do to try to help our clients, people make their own choices. It took me a long time to learn this.

Growing up I had a lot of guilt if I couldn't solve all of our family problems. Through the support of my husband, I came to realize, "There's nothing wrong with helping, but when helping hurts you, you can't keep helping others."

He said, "All this time, money, and energy that you're investing in your extended family, you're not giving to your own kids or giving to me as your husband." When he told me this, it helped me recognize times that I was constantly fixing problems for my extended family instead of allowing them to be responsible for their own lives.

> *Just like in my extended family, chaos shows up in our agency every day . . . I'm mindful of my tendency to take on a protective "fixer" role.*

That was a turning point that helped me to create boundaries with my extended family and as a leader with my employees and clients.

Just like in my extended family, chaos shows up in our agency every day. Whether it's with our clients or with a staff member, I'm mindful of my tendency to take on a protective "fixer" role. Now, instead of being part of and consumed by the chaos, as I was in my family upbringing, I see what's happening, step back, and equip people to *take care of themselves,* instead of me doing it for them.

I still bring order out of chaos; however, I've changed my conflict pattern by removing myself as the fixer. I strive daily to figure out that fine line between offering alternatives from violence, while allowing people to make their own choices. Most importantly, I want people to know there is a way out and I'm living proof!

Productive Conflict Management Strategies

1. Look at Your Past in Order to Understand How It Brings You to Where You Are Today.

If it weren't for all the experiences I had, I wouldn't be the person I am today. If we look at how we're able to overcome things within our own family dynamics, it becomes very easy to apply the lessons from those experiences to situations at work. Because the workplace is still groups of people working together or working against each other—and how we've been able to prevail within our own families is the way that we can prevail at work.

2. When in Conflict, Consider What Brings Other People to How and Where They Are Today.

Although I had a chaotic upbringing, I know other people who had much worse situations. Have empathy for why people behave the way they do. That doesn't mean you let them off the hook for their behavior. It's about having the compassion to understand that people often behave in negative ways because that's all they know.

3. Find Those People Who Inspire You to Bring Out Your Best.

Regardless of your upbringing, find people who will see your strengths, hold you accountable, and inspire you to be your best. That's what the Catholic nuns and my maternal grandmother did for me.

4. Be Aware of the Ways Culture Is a Factor in How Conflict Is Dealt with in the Workplace.

Different cultures have very different ways of dealing with conflict. It's important as a leader to try to understand these differences, which will help you manage conflicts more effectively—especially if you have a diverse workforce.

5. Take Time to Take Care of Yourself.

I recognize that as a leader, there are days when demands and problems are hitting me and I'm having a pretty bad day. I excuse myself and take a moment because I know I'm not going to solve anything by not being professional or considerate of other people. I take some time to set boundaries with my staff, to let them know I'm in my office and I need some time to be quiet so I can take control of my emotions, take care of myself, and come back better centered, focused, and energized.

6. Remove Yourself from Being the "Fixer" of Other People's Problems.

Instead of trying to fix other people's problems, step back and equip people to take responsibility for themselves. You will be a more effective leader if you set boundaries and stay out of joining the reactivity of others.

The Family Factor:
Let People Do What They're
Capable of Doing for Themselves

Throughout Maria's upbringing, she witnessed violence, alcoholism, and abuse as a way of solving problems. When she had her first child at age 16, she started her journey of changing her family conflict pattern driven by one motivation: "I didn't want to be like my parents." As a result, she became a fixer—trying to take responsibility for and resolve everyone's problems.

What many leaders don't realize is that becoming a fixer is their Family Factor. Like Maria, they became fixers in the workplace because of events in their upbringing.

Harriet Lerner in her classic book *The Dance of Anger* states:

> *We are never the first in our family to wrestle with a problem, although it may feel that way. All of us inherit the unsolved problems of our past and whatever we are struggling with has its legacy in the struggles of prior generations. If we do not know about our own family history, we are more likely to repeat past patterns or mindlessly rebel against them without much clarity about who we really are, how we are similar to and different from other family members, and how we might proceed in our own life.*

Through self-awareness, the role-modeling of her grandmother, her education, the support of her husband, and her own pertinacity, Maria was acutely aware of her family's unsolved problems. She was also aware of how she naturally took on the role of fixer in the family because of the struggles of prior generations of violent men and submissive women.

The role of the fixer in the family is what Harriett Lerner refers to as the "overfunctioner." This person deals with the anxiety in the family system by enabling, advising, rescuing, and taking charge of those in the family who are "underfunctioners." "Underfunctioning" occurs when people deal with anxiety by allowing others in the family to take care of them in any situation.

In the workplace, there are many leaders who are fixers. They're naturally drawn to taking charge, to being proactive and productive. This tendency, however, can lead them to be overfunctioners—taking over activities or decisions that should be the responsibilities of those they lead. This overfunctioning turns the managers and employees below them into underfunctioners, ready to follow their leaders without questioning or even thinking. The spiral of overfunctioning and underfunctioning is evident in conflict situations, when leaders immediately step in to fix the situation rather than allow people to work through their conflict.

The following chart provides examples of feedback you may have been given from others if you're an overfunctioner and how you can change.

As an overfunctioner, I've been told:	What you can do about being an overfunctioner:
I can be perceived as bossy and micromanage people.	Ask for other's opinions before sharing yours. Listen without interrupting. Ask questions with curiosity.
I come across as arrogant and like a know-it-all.	Admit mistakes. Ask for help.
People are afraid to speak up with new ideas because I make condescending comments about the ideas and/or people in front of others.	Be aware of your tone of voice such as speaking down to people with a condescending tone. Take a genuine interest in people by looking at them when they're speaking. Give feedback privately.

This second chart provides examples of feedback you may have been given from others if you're an underfunctioner and how you can change.

As an underfunctioner, I've been told:	What you can do about being an underfunctioner:
When I don't speak up with ideas when a decision needs to be made, I come across as disinterested.	Give your opinion and suggestions, even if you feel uncomfortable or fear being criticized.
When faced with a problem, I look to others to tell me what to do instead of offering solutions.	Take the initiative with solutions when problems arise, even if you're not sure if what you're suggesting will work out.
When faced with a problem, I can't be trusted to make sure a problem is resolved.	Follow-up to make sure problems are resolved and projects are finished.
My staff doesn't trust me as their leader to look out for them to the higher ups.	Tell my employees what I'm doing to be an advocate for them and give regular updates.

One way to recognize this Family Factor of overfunctioning is through the "Get Your Own Kleenex®" test.

Get Your Own Kleenex

Shortly after I was hired in my first leadership position, I encountered an office culture of silence and secrets. I was excluded from meetings and information, which prevented me from fully performing my job. Despite my attempts to get direct answers from my boss, the lack of communication continued and started to take a toll on my confidence. In order to deal with the stress and grow as a leader, I joined a therapy group composed of other professionals (doctors, teachers, nurses, lawyers, and project managers) who also valued personal growth. We developed a special bond of support and encouragement by being transparent about work and life struggles without being "fixers" to one another.

Besides the typical group rules of confidentiality, etc., we followed a rule of getting your own Kleenex. We were free to express emotion, but if someone needed a Kleenex, he or she needed to get one from the box that was easily accessible.

The reason for the "Get Your Own Kleenex" rule relates to the overfunctioner/underfunctioner roles.

When people show emotion, it's common to pass them a Kleenex without them asking for one. It's considered being courteous, a kind gesture.

The "Get Your Own Kleenex" concept is intended to stop fixers and those with a tendency to be overfunctioners from doing for others what they're capable of doing for themselves, in this case, getting their own Kleenex. It allows for someone who leans toward being an underfunctioner to be responsible for themselves.

Our therapist said in essence, "The Kleenex is available if you want them. It's your responsibility to take care of yourself. I won't do something for you that you're capable of doing . . . even if it's as simple as getting your own Kleenex."

This simple group "rule" taught us several valuable lessons:

- How to be present with someone who is showing emotion without fixing

- Noticing the urge to want to help someone else and take charge of the situation (pass the Kleenex)

- Feeling emotions that may be uncomfortable, including silence

- Being responsible for handling your own emotions (getting your own Kleenex)

Another group "rule" was no advice-giving. Since many over-functioners tend to readily give advice, this rule helped us to notice the tendency to fix another's problems. It also allowed space for underfunctioners to figure problems out on their own.

Maria's story underscores how both overfunctioners and underfunctioners basically have the same problem: they both need one another. If you have one, you have the other. Overfunctioners need underfunctioners to not be responsible and underfunctioners need overfunctioners to take care of them.

As a leader, if you are overfunctioning and tend to pick up the pieces for your employees, you are doing them a disservice. You are teaching them to underfunction.

As a leader, if you are underfunctioning and your employees may be picking up the pieces for you, covering for you in some way, they are doing you a disservice. They are teaching you to not be responsible.

Maria recognized she was overfunctioning as the family fixer. By removing herself from this role, she was able to be more accessible for her own family and allow space for her extended family to be responsible for their own choices and life. She's also applied this same skill to her role as a leader.

When a team or organizational system is out of balance with overfunctioners and underfunctioners, it becomes a breeding ground for resentment, anger, gossip, and many other dysfunctions. The goal as a leader is to create an environment where everyone functions to their full capability, taking responsibility for their words, behaviors, and actions: where everyone gets their own Kleenex.

Reference

Lerner, Harriet. *The Dance of Anger: A Woman's Guide To Changing The Patterns Of Intimate Relationships.* New York: HarperCollins, 1985.

Self-Reflection Questions

1. In what ways do you relate to Maria's role of overfunctioning as the "fixer" through advising, rescuing, or in some other way taking charge when others underfunction?

2. In what ways might you be underfunctioning, i.e., afraid to speak up with your ideas?

3. List examples where you can start allowing others to take responsibility for their actions and get their own Kleenex.

4. When you encounter employees, co-workers, or clients of another culture, what adjustments could you make to keep the lines of communication open and minimize conflict?

5. Maria became aware that when she was overfunctioning and focused on fixing others' problems, it took time and attention away from her own family. In what ways might your work or focus on other people's problems be taking you away from your own family, friends, and personal life?

The fact is, employees cannot make breakthroughs if they can't openly and honestly disagree with their peers and their leader. Indeed, great leaders don't just permit conflict; they actively try to elicit it from reluctant employees as well.

—Patrick Lencioni

CHAPTER TWO

John's Story
"I Wouldn't Make A Good 'Undercover Boss'"

Chapter Summary: As a senior leader, John specializes in transforming struggling corporations, making them viable and sustainably profitable while forging a culture of trust, respect, and accountability. His story reveals how someone who has a very stable upbringing with minimal exposure to conflict may develop the belief that all conflict is bad. John shares how he turned around his tendency to avoid conflict through utilizing what he learned from his parents—lessons that empowered him to develop productive conflict management skills as a leader. His story is a tribute to the influence of his parents on his leadership success—a success built on his showing a genuine interest in his employees. He says he wouldn't make a good "Undercover Boss" because his employees would recognize him, even wearing a disguise, from their interactions with him and how he demonstrates he cares about them.

Growing Up in Humble Beginnings

The first time I can recall not having to share a bed was when I went away to college. I grew up in a blue-collar family living in a 900 sq. ft. house with my parents and two younger siblings. Dad was a hard-working welder who worked his way up in the labor union from an apprentice to a supervisor. Mom never worked outside the home and made sure we were healthy, nourished, and loved. I was the first in our family to attend and graduate from college.

Dad didn't have paid vacations so we often did what's today called "staycations." We'd go fishing or to a baseball game, doing the kind of things that a kid remembers as quality family time.

We didn't have much conflict growing up, virtually none. Early in my career, I abhorred conflict because I didn't have a strong base of experience to draw upon and didn't understand how to handle it well. If conflict arose, I would try to find common ground and bridge the gap by emphasizing points of agreement. If common ground didn't exist, I would try to shut down the conflict and move on. I truly believed that conflict was bad because of my minimal exposure to conflict growing up.

From Conflict Avoidance to Productive Conflict Management Skills

I didn't really appreciate the role of productive conflict in business until about 15 years ago. It was in reading a landmark book at the time—*The Five Dysfunctions of a Team* by Patrick Lencioni—that I realized the value of how conflict can be productive. After reading and embracing the model put forth by Lencioni, I became acutely aware that fear of conflict was a dysfunction that was limiting my team's potential. I've since become a catalyst for productive conflict, which includes soliciting alternative points of view. I now realize that the best ideas should always win out regardless of their source and that without productive conflict you rarely arrive at the best ideas.

I really embraced Lencioni's concept that having productive conflict starts with a foundation of trust. I've used that model in every organization I've worked with since reading his book, because I wholeheartedly believe in it. It doesn't matter who has the ideas, and sometimes they're synergistic, but they're usually better than any one person could have come up with alone.

How My Family Shows Up in My Office

My parents were kind and caring people who taught us discipline and values. They were involved in our lives as kids—not just in giving us their time—but more importantly, in giving their attention to each of us kids as individuals. I remember times when my dad didn't have work locally, and he'd be away for weeks at a time

> *My family, in particular my parents, show up every day in my office through my leadership style.*

in order to provide for the family. Even when he was away, he kept in touch with us and we knew he'd be back. Mom took care of things at home and maintained a sense of normalcy. My parents showed me what it's like when couples work together as a team. They were also very intentional about staying in touch with extended family. Some of my best memories are playing with my cousins and sitting around the table at my grandparents' house listening to family stories. I cherished those times with family.

My family, in particular my parents, show up every day in my office through my leadership style. Because of the genuine interest my parents took in my siblings and me, that's how I relate to those with whom I work.

As my dad tells me, "Son, you don't have to prove to your employees how smart you are. They know you're smart because they wouldn't have chosen you to do this job if you weren't smart. That doesn't matter. You've got to show them that you care about them."

I wouldn't make a good "Undercover Boss" because I put my dad's wisdom into practice. I interact with our employees on a regular basis. I don't have to go undercover in a disguise to find out how they're doing or what their perceptions are of the company. I hear it directly from them because I take a personal interest in them like my parents did in me, asking more questions, then providing answers and showing I genuinely care about them. We work together, we laugh together, we celebrate together, and we pray together.

I also earn their trust because I am not afraid to admit mistakes—another lesson that my parents taught me. I remember as a teenager, I played in an all-star baseball game and I struck out. I was upset that I let my team down. After the game, my dad shared with me a similar situation when he was in the Army. Dad was playing on a select team and they lost 1-0 because he had made an error in the field.

When I was beating myself up for not helping my team, Dad shared that story with me. He said, "Hey, I've walked in your shoes, I've lived that life lesson that you're trying to live now, son, and I came out okay. You will too."

Today, as a leader, I admit mistakes to my team because my dad modeled this to me. His example gave me confidence to be vulnerable and in turn my vulnerability gives others permission to share their mistakes.

Treating Employees as Individuals

My parents had a knack for motivating my siblings and me based on our individual temperament. While we had consistent rules and privileges that applied to all of us, my parents figured out what motivated us as individuals.

In the same way, I recognize that what inspires employees in the factory will be different than what inspires and motivates the professional staff at the corporate office or the staff in the field. As a leader, it's figuring out how to personalize motivation, and that's what my dad does really well.

Whenever I start a new job, my dad writes me letters to encourage me. He'll remind me about what's most important, like putting people first. He's also written poems to us and other family members after a milestone event like a graduation. He started writing me letters about 20 years ago, when I first began to have people responsibilities in my job, and people counting on me. Up until then he imparted his words of wisdom as part of our conversations.

As a leader, I'm intentional about writing personalized notes to employees about the qualities I appreciate about them and to acknowledge the efforts they make for our company.

Another leadership lesson I learned from my dad is the importance of getting involved. Dad would often tell us kids "you have no right to complain if you choose to stand on the sidelines."

When I was growing up, we didn't have any sports programs at the grade school I attended. I loved basketball. It was one of my favorite pastimes, and Dad knew that.

Instead of waiting for the school to develop an athletic program, my dad became the athletic director at the school, and built the sports programs out of nothing. He raised the money and got his friends together to set up the basketball program. They installed the hoops and purchased other necessary equipment so we could have a basketball program. That program has continued for 35 years and was based on my dad's vision. That's leadership: rolling up your sleeves and making things happen, rather than waiting for others to do it. I don't think even the best graduate schools in the country teach you the essence of what leadership is all about and the temperament that's required to be an effective leader. I ultimately learned leadership from what my dad modeled.

The manufacturing industry is a tough business. There's nothing elegant about what we do, it's just hard work. I appreciate the people on the factory floor who make things happen. Those women and men leave their homes at 4:15 in the morning each and every day to come to the factory and put in a good day's work. My parents modeled the importance of a solid work ethic and appreciating people for what they do. They taught us to express thanks and never take anything or anyone for granted.

I hope that's why there's confidence in me when I go into organizations as an unknown leader to turn around a business that is on a downhill slide. I don't ask employees to do anything that I wouldn't do. I want to learn from them and I want to solicit and listen to their ideas. Every situation is unique; there are no cookie-cutter approaches to turnarounds of under-performing businesses. That's not management-speak that I picked up when I went to graduate school or read in a book. That's my parents; that's what they taught us. I have all these inspirational quotes going around in my head that my parents said to me as a youngster:

- *A good day's work for a good day's pay.*

- *Promises made are promises kept.*

- *Don't be a quitter because you'll set yourself up for quitting your whole life, and giving in when things are tough.*

- *You have no right to complain if you choose to stand on the sidelines.*

- *Get involved and make a difference.*

- *Talent will only take you so far, it's your effort, it's your attitude—those are the only things you can control.*

- *Son, don't prove how smart you are, show them that you care.*

These are the types of principles my parents instilled in us as kids, and I still believe in them today.

Productive Conflict Management Strategies

1. Be Intentional in Learning Productive Conflict Management Skills.

As a leader, it was actually a strength, that I wasn't exposed to much conflict as a kid. I grew up in a very stable home that gave me a secure base from which to develop into a strong leader. The challenge was that I didn't have the skills to manage conflict well. I was uncomfortable with conflict and tended to avoid it because I didn't know how to handle it. But I made the decision to turn the challenge into an opportunity by learning productive conflict management skills.

2. Treat Your Employees with Dignity and Get to Know Them as Individuals.

Learn about your employees' lives, their interests, and their families, beyond what they do as an employee. Never ask people to do something you wouldn't do yourself.

When there are employee behavior or performance issues that need to be addressed, employees tend to be more receptive when I speak with them because of the personal interest I've shown them, and the relationship we have built leading up to the conversation.

3. Admit Your Mistakes.

Making mistakes is how we learn.

Making mistakes is a big part of being a leader because leadership is about taking risks. I've tried a lot of things and not all have been successful. I go into situations acknowledging some things won't work. From the outset, we just don't know which business initiatives will work and which won't. But if we keep trying and apply what we have learned from our mistakes, we will achieve improved results.

Being willing to admit my mistakes has prevented conflict and difficult conversations from escalating. It shows my employees I'm human, too, and I take responsibility for my actions.

4. Write Personalized, Handwritten Notes to Your Employees.

Just like treating your employees with dignity, writing personalized notes acknowledges the uniqueness of each person and demonstrates that you care.

When differences and conflict occur, if people know you sincerely care about them, trust develops. When trust is in the relationship, conflict can more readily be resolved. Trust is the foundation of all productive relationships.

5. Get Involved and Make a Difference.

Dad modeled getting involved in the work of making things happen. In the same way, when it comes to resolving conflict, leaders need to get involved in working through differences and having difficult conversations. Productive conflict takes effort and intentionality. It's the willingness to go first, to initiate and work through difficult conversations . . . not waiting for others to make a difference.

6. Face Challenges and Conflict as Temporary, Instead of Permanent.

When my parents went through tough times, like when my dad was in another country for weeks on end in order to find work, they both had the attitude that this is only temporary. They didn't view it as anything that would debilitate our family permanently. They focused on the importance of effort and attitude because those are the things you can control. You can't control how much talent you have, how smart you are, but you have 100 percent control over the effort you're going to put into something and the attitude you're going to bring to it every day.

Just like my parents' attitude set the tone for our family, my attitude as a leader sets the tone for our organizational culture, including how we address conflict.

7. Simplify What You Want People to Do.

Whether you're putting together a proposal or a business strategy, make it simple so people can understand what's expected of them. No one can buy into it, support it, or believe in it unless they can understand it.

Much conflict can be avoided by having mutually agreed-upon expectations that are discussed upfront. When employees are clear on what's expected of them, the resources available to them, and timeliness, there's less likelihood of conflict and more opportunity to create win-win solutions.

8. Minimize Conflict When Introducing Change by Acknowledging Change Is Hard, Takes Courage, and Is A Choice.

When I first start working with an underperforming company to turn it around, I explain to people that you can be in one of three camps regarding how you'll deal with change:

Fearful: View change as threatening because things could get worse;

Hopeful: View change as encouraging because things could get better;

Confident: View change as inspiring because the challenge exists to improve the way things are.

My job as a leader is to inspire the fearful to become hopeful and give the change we are introducing a chance. If people are hopeful, ideally that's a stepping stone to confidence. I want our employees to know I understand it's normal to have fear around change. If I don't let them know I understand how hard change is, the change could alienate people and lead to conflict and resistance. I make a big deal of recognizing the courage it takes to change.

It's one thing to initiate change, it's another thing to sustain it. If people are going to buy into change, they need to know they have a choice. I have worked with some companies who bring me in because they recognize the need for change in order for their company to stay viable. However, when it comes time to actually implement change, some owners resist it, as it takes them out of their comfort zone.

The confidence my parents instilled has enabled me to walk away when people choose not to change. The worst thing you can do as a leader is to force change upon someone who doesn't want to change. It doesn't make them a bad person; change is a choice that not everyone is willing to make.

The Family Factor:
Become a Catalyst for Productive Conflict

John's upbringing gave him a secure base of self-worth. From childhood on, he received positive messages about his value as a person and the belief that he had the inner resources to handle life's challenges. The Family Factor for John was that the absence of conflict in his life instilled in him the sense that any conflict was destructive and needed to be avoided at all costs. Eventually he began to recognize the potential for *productive* conflict, and from his foundation of security and self-worth, he was able to explore how to introduce productive conflict in the workplace.

Leadership is a culmination of life experiences and intentional development efforts.

In recent years, research in the field of neuroscience and attachment theory has provided a deeper understanding of the importance of relationships in the workplace. George Kohlrieser and co-authors Susan Goldsworthy and Duncan Coombe state the following in their book, *Care to Dare: Unleashing Astonishing Potential Through Secure Base Leadership.*

> *Leadership is a culmination of life experiences and intentional development efforts. Secure Base Leaders recognize the power of their past and fully understand how the history of their beliefs, habits, and relationship patterns impacts their leadership. The past includes both positive, rich experiences and negative experiences from*

which leaders have learned. Your life story brings your attention to the people, experiences, and events that shaped you and it prepares you to make a conscious choice about the secure bases you want in your life going forward.

From a neuroscience perspective, John's parents provided consistent emotional support that gave John a solid foundation—or "secure base," in the terms of the authors—on which to stand. From this relationship bond with his parents, John's brain developed neurological connections that fostered his capability to regulate his emotions.

When John realized how much he avoided conflict—in his words "abhorred" it—he tapped into his internal strength and sense of security from his upbringing to recognize the need to grow in how he handled conflict, and to learn skills that were unfamiliar to him. By focusing on the benefit of helping his team develop their potential and using the Lencioni model as his navigation guide, he rewired his brain from conflict avoidance to productive conflict.

As he developed a career specialty of turning around failing companies, he has continued to extend the secure attachment he received from his parents to leaders and employees who are in a state of fear: fear of the unknown, of what will happen to the company under John's leadership, of whether they will still have a job—and if they do, how the changes under John's leadership will affect them.

When John goes into companies, he establishes himself as a secure base by acknowledging employee fear(s) of change up front, as well as acknowledging that he is upsetting the status quo. If the company is going to become viable again and employee jobs retained, he recognizes that his role is not just turning around a company financially, but also to guide employees through their fear of the unknown and attachment to how things used to be.

While on a practical level John follows Patrick Lencioni's model of productive conflict, he believes his parents are in his office every day as the true inspiration for how he interacts with employees on a human level. From taking a personal interest in employees through face-to-face conversations, to acknowledging an employee's uniqueness in handwritten notes, John's family legacy provides riches that can't be measured on a spreadsheet.

References

Kohlrieser, George, Susan Goldsworthy, Susan and Duncan Coombe. *Care to Dare: Unleashing Astonishing Potential Through Secure Base Leadership.* San Francisco, CA: John Wiley & Sons, 2012.

Lencioni, Patrick. *The Five Dysfunctions of a Team: A Leadership Fable.* San Francisco, CA: Jossey-Bass, a Wiley Imprint, 2002.

Self-Reflection Questions

1. In what ways do you relate to John's original perspective that "all conflict was bad and had to be avoided"?

2. How has conflict avoidance limited your team's potential and innovative ideas?

3. What inspirational quotes did you receive in your upbringing that you apply to how you show up at work or interact with co-workers, employees, and your boss?

4. Who has been a positive role model to you in how conflict is dealt with? How have they inspired you?

5. Which of John's productive conflict management strategies will you implement with your employees? When?

When you show deep empathy toward others, their defensive energy goes down, and positive energy replaces it. That's when you can get more creative in solving problems.

—Stephen Covey

CHAPTER THREE

June's Story
A Journey From Brutality To
Empathy And Emotional Intelligence

Chapter Summary: June grew up in an alcoholic, volatile family. It wasn't unusual for police to show up at the family home to break up a fistfight or for a drug or burglary raid. As June was climbing the corporate ladder, she became an alcoholic. Eventually she got sober and turned her life around. Her story reveals her determination and pertinacity to change her family conflict pattern by rejecting the brutality modeled in her childhood and choosing, instead, a leadership style driven by empathy.

My Upbringing in Three Words: Alcohol, Conflict, and Chaos

My childhood was very chaotic, especially during my teen years. It wasn't unusual to have physical fistfights and police coming to the house for raids related to drugs and burglaries, due to one of my brothers.

Growing up with five siblings, the family house dynamic was a constant shouting match, ending with one person leaving the room and nothing getting resolved. Dad was an alcoholic and Mom pretended it wasn't happening. Conflict was ignored, so if there were opposing views or a big argument one night, the next day you pretended it never happened. Issues were never discussed, and no attempt was made to understand the other person's point of view. Instead, we tended to have a kind of hierarchy: whoever thought they were the stronger or dominant person yelled at the subservient or less dominant person. My dad typically yelled at my mother, or one brother in particular would yell at the other one. Whoever yelled the most, won. When they disagreed, Dad bullied his way through, and Mom avoided addressing the conflict. Neither approach worked.

Dad got sober when I was seven years old, after years of promising to stop drinking. Even when Dad was sober, he reverted back to the angry blustering and didn't really change his behavior. He began drinking again when I was in my late teens, and then stopped again when I was in my early 20s.

My role in the family was like a rebel against the family norms of chaos. In some ways I bullied my way through like Dad, but it was my way to be heard amidst all the fighting. I was the only one in the family who would stand up to Dad and confront him about his drinking. I remember when I was about ten years old, my dad kicked over a trash basket when he was drinking and then told my brother to pick it up. I said he shouldn't have to pick it up because he didn't kick it over. I told Dad he should pick it up because he kicked it over. My dad yelled at me, "You take that back" and I wouldn't. He then spanked me and kept saying, "You take that back," but I wouldn't. He kept spanking me to the point I couldn't even feel my butt anymore. Even though I was numb from him hitting me, I never took it back, challenging him to be responsible. My brother ended up picking up the trash basket because he wasn't going to put himself through what he saw happening to me.

> *My role in the family was like a rebel against the family norms of chaos. I was the only one in the family who would stand up to Dad and confront him about his drinking.*

Another incident with my dad happened when he blamed the family bankruptcy on a surgery that I needed as a child. I didn't talk to my dad for at least six months after that. He never apologized. My mom assured me the bankruptcy wasn't my fault.

As a kid, I was often teased at school. Neither of my parents were nurturing about it. Instead, they encouraged me to fight back and beat up the kids who were saying mean things to me. I learned to take care of myself and was looked at as the stable, go-to person in the family—the one who brought order out of the chaos.

I never invited friends to come over to my house growing up because of the yelling and alcoholism. It's like we were always hiding so that no one could see the family chaos. Once I stayed at a friend's house overnight and her parents kissed her goodnight and gave her a hug. I asked her, "Why did they do that?" My friend said, "We do that every night." I had no idea that families showed affection; the only physical contact in my family was through hitting. There was no loving, hugging, or positive emotions shown. As an adult, it took me well into my 20s to accept a friendly hug because of how we were raised, and it was uncomfortable. It also took me years to have a party to let people in my house, because growing up, we never had people over.

How My Family Shows Up in My Office

My family upbringing left me without the emotional intelligence skills and empathy needed to be an effective leader.

I had an employee who came into work one day and said he was late because his girlfriend's pet had died. I said, "That's just not a good enough reason. You need to be here on time." A colleague who'd heard the conversation pulled me aside at lunch and commented that I wasn't very empathetic to my employee when he told me his grandmother had died. I said, "His grandmother didn't die; it was his girlfriend's pet!" I felt justified in my position that the death of a pet was not an excuse for coming to work late.

Years later, after I lost one of my own pets, I realized how emotional it was to lose a pet. It brought me back to that day that I told my employee he shouldn't be late because his girlfriend's pet died. I thought, "That was so insensitive on your part, June."

This learning took me years to figure out because we didn't have emotional expression in my family. It took a long time for me to give people the right to be late, for reasons other than what I had originally thought were legitimate reasons—such as a physical illness. I learned that emotions also impact work: if a person is not emotionally able to function, they shouldn't be at work.

Another legacy of my chaotic family upbringing was accepting brutally negative situations that most people would never accept.

I worked at a company for nine years with the promise of receiving a significant amount of money when my company stock options hit. During this time, I endured working for a boss who would yell and swear at me. During board presentations, it wasn't unusual for him to say, "Sit (expletive) down till you know what you're talking about." Every quarter I would have to present to the board and for two weeks leading up to my presentation, I had intestinal problems knowing I would be verbally ripped to shreds. Because that's what the CEO thought was appropriate to do to motivate people. It was a brutal company and yet, because I had so many stock options, I kept telling myself I would leave as soon as the stock options went big.

When the market was turning, I realized I wasn't going to get a big financial gain. I thought, "It's not worth the money." I felt like I was prostituting myself for stock to stay at this company, and deep down, I knew I couldn't do this anymore. I needed a better quality of life and I began looking for another job.

I was offered a management position with another company right away. This meant I would go from a director position with a lucrative compensation, to no longer being the top dog. Everything in me said that if I left my prestigious position (even though it was abusive), I was going to have to start my career all over!

Then I realized I was questioning whether to leave out of fear of the unknown. I didn't know what to expect at the new job. The brutal way I was being treated—being verbally raked over the coals—was familiar to me. I was used to being treated with abuse and I stayed for the promise of the stock options. Just like, deep down, I'd always hoped for love, attention, and acceptance in my family. I stayed with that company for as long as I did because the way I was treated was so similar to my family upbringing. My family was in my office.

I finally decided to leave the brutal company when I realized I was worthy of being treated better than how I was being treated.

Somewhat ironically, I did learn one lesson from my mother that helped me when, early in my career, I was traveling extensively. I did a lot of travel to one country where the culture norm is to avoid addressing problems directly. People cover for coworkers; you never "out" anyone. Once I was trying to figure out why a project didn't happen on time. Then I realized, nobody's going to tell me!

That conflict style was familiar to me; it mirrored how my mom avoided confronting the problem of my dad's drinking. Even though I wanted to get to the bottom of the problem, once I understood the norms of how this particular culture worked (to cover it up), I joined the system by letting people off the hook and we moved forward with the project.

When I made this connection for myself, I understood what was happening. Just like our family dynamics, we all come from different backgrounds and we have to learn to work with each other regardless of whether we agree or not. In order for work to get done in different cultures, respecting differences and joining the system is sometimes the best thing we can do.

How I Changed My Family Pattern to Become a Better Leader

I never wanted to believe that because I was raised in conflict, chaos, and unpredictability that I needed to be that way. My mom often said she "was raised this way" (to be an avoider), meaning she couldn't change. I've always believed a person can choose to change behaviors. I didn't always know how to do it, but there were three major events that were the catalysts for how, as an adult, I changed my behavior and my family patterns: Sobriety, Therapy, and Emotional Intelligence Skills.

Getting Sober

What prompted my sobriety was reading an article about the impact of alcoholism on a family. After reading it, I called my company's Employee Assistance Program (EAP) and said I'd like to see a counselor to understand this better. Within a few weeks, the counselor asked me about my own drinking. At that point, I was drinking almost daily and having blackouts. I didn't think anything of it, it was normal for me. The counselor said, "That's a sure sign of an alcoholic," and I said, "No, I don't think this pertains to me."

A few days later I was talking to a friend about what the counselor said and the possibility that I could be an alcoholic. Without skipping a beat he said, "I could have told you that!" I said, "Why didn't you tell me?" and he said, "You weren't ready to hear it yet. I've known it for ten years! My brother is an alcoholic, so I get it. I see the same behaviors in you that I see in him."

From my friend's candor, I was able to say the words "I'm an alcoholic" for the first time with someone I felt safe with. What kept me sober was realizing I was sick and tired of using drinking to cover up my emotions and blocking out everything that happened in my upbringing. I also just didn't like myself.

Getting sober allowed the foundation for the introspection to understand the impact of all the chaos growing up, and how it affected both my personal and professional life. I wouldn't be the person or leader I am today if I hadn't made the choice to work on myself and see that I had alternatives other than drinking every day.

Getting Therapy

Through therapy I learned to be more accepting of emotions and accepting that decisions weren't all or nothing. That allowed me to be introspective—to look at myself and to accept myself. And I learned at the same time that not every decision in life is a business decision. To take into consideration how people feel (including me) was a huge learning experience for me!

What was especially transformative for me in therapy was learning how most of my own drinking was done to block out the painful memories and messages from my upbringing. I learned how I used drinking to calm down emotionally.

A big eye opener for me was realizing that when I got in people's faces with anger, whether in my personal or professional life, they didn't take me seriously. All they could see was my anger and aggression. My message got lost in the emotion and the real problem didn't get addressed. They just knew somebody got really pissed off!

It was a new concept for me that when people don't feel heard, it affects the relationship. I was used to being right, making decisions, and moving on. I learned how my behavior was based in fear, and being angry was the way I stayed safe to make sure I got ahead. I also learned I was valuable as a person without having to prove myself by having the last word.

Emotional Intelligence Skills

Getting sober and attending therapy gave me the insight and the tools to change behaviors that weren't working for me in my personal life. Fortunately, I worked for a company that offered emotional intelligence classes that helped me recognize how unknowingly my overly aggressive behaviors were undermining my leadership style. This was back in the '90s, so it was very progressive for an employer to recognize how enhancing interpersonal skills and a leader's management style could benefit the company's bottom-line results.

I attended several trainings through my employer, but one, in particular, stands out to me with two key takeaways for my growth as a leader.

The first takeaway was in a class where there were two of us that were on the aggressive side. We tended to bowl over people. The other eight people in the class were more on the timid side and weren't very assertive. The two of us had to learn how to tame ourselves down and the others had to learn how to speak up. I think that was a very important learning experience for me to see the contrast in leadership styles and how we could learn from one another.

For example, instead of always stating the way we're going to do something, I learned the importance of letting other people have an opinion and having more of a conversation or a dialogue. And I learned to let people try things. If they failed, they would learn from it. If I always told them what to do, the employee would never learn and we wouldn't work as well as a team.

I realized if I wanted my life and leadership to be better, I needed to learn the difference between "aggressive" and "assertive." I was aggressive, not assertive. When you're aggressive, your message isn't heard. All others hear is the emotion and that shuts people down. When you're assertive, you're asking for what you want or stating a fact, and not wrapping it up in either bullying or "I'm right, you're wrong."

The second big takeaway I took from this class happened when one of the facilitators asked me, "Tell me about your background?" After telling her how I grew up in a family that was constantly fighting and leaving, and how I learned to bully my way through to be heard, the facilitator said something that has stuck with me since the moment she said it: "You can quit running now. You've made it out of the house, you're okay now, and you're safe. You don't need to run anymore."

Without realizing it, I had learned to become very much like my dad, both as a person and as a leader. My aggressive leadership style was limiting my effectiveness. Yet, I wasn't doing it intentionally. My behavior was driven by how, in my family, I spoke up and took charge in order to bring calm out of the chaos and stay safe.

> *My behavior was driven by how, in my family, I spoke up and took charge in order to bring calm out of the chaos and stay safe.*

The words the training facilitator said to me were freeing. Her words resonated with me: I didn't need to prove myself to anybody. I could stop bullying my way with my aggressiveness because I had survived my family—I was out of the house, safe and okay. I didn't need to run from the chaos in the family anymore. I was successful in my own right. That was life-changing for me.

Climbing Back Up the Ladder

It was through getting sober and gaining self-awareness in therapy that I got to the root of why I had stayed so long in that brutal company. Bottom-line: quality of life wins over materialistic possessions—and I faced the fears of the unknown rather than stay with the chaos and abuse of what was familiar to me.

Now many years later, I've worked my way back up the corporate ladder in a high-tech electronics company and earned the money and more than what I had left behind. I'm grateful for how sobriety, therapy, and the skills I've learned through employer trainings have empowered me: to channel my determination and tenacity in order to face and overcome the fears that were rooted in my upbringing!

Productive Conflict Management Strategies

1. Find Out What Motivates People and Have Empathy.

There is more trust and respect in the workplace if you learn to understand what motivates each person and what is important for them—not for you. Some people are motivated by being heard.

Being open to listen to people and being flexible to adapt your leadership style based on what motivates different people can make the difference between keeping and losing dedicated employees.

It wasn't until the loss of my own pet, for example, that I learned to have empathy for the emotional impact of loss or other events in my employees' lives. Having empathy for my employees has made me a better leader, and in turn, created more productive employees.

2. Take Advantage of Leadership Development Training.

Sometimes leaders discount the impact of how their behavior influences employees. Not only did the training sessions I referenced above help me to be less aggressive and work through conflict more effectively as a leader, they also helped in how I interacted with other world cultures.

In the early years of my career, I frequently traveled internationally. My company also sent me to culture awareness training so I could learn how to effectively interact with different world cultures.

3. Encourage the "Steady Eddy's" and Ignore Bad Behavior.

I call the employee whose behavior is positive and consistent, the "Steady Eddy."

As a leader, it's so easy to get caught up in the employee exhibiting bad behavior and reward the bad behavior by giving all your attention to the employee who's being negative. That's what happened in my family: much of the attention was on the trouble my brothers were getting into. As a result, my other siblings and me, who weren't getting into trouble but were still struggling, often got overlooked.

Spend time helping the positive Steady Eddies to develop. There's room for everybody. Support people to do the best they can do. Even if your Steady Eddies are lower performers, work with them to develop their skill set and get better, instead of penalizing them. After trying to develop their skills, you might find they're not in the right job; then move them on, because it's not right for anybody to keep an underperformer. At least give them a chance.

4. When Conflict Happens, Ask the Question, "How Did We Get to This Point?"

I can make myself crazy when everything goes haywire and a bunch of things happen all at once.

Instead, taking time to ask the question, "How did we get to this point?" helps us recognize that we all have skin in the game: we all play a part in creating the conflict, and we all must play a part toward resolving the conflict. That way, everyone provides input about what they think we should do: we're all equals, and together we'll figure out a solution.

5. Be Prepared for Pushback from Upper Management.

When I became more collaborative as a leader and less directive, my upper management team didn't like it.

Creating learning experiences for people sometimes adds more time to get projects done instead of just telling people what to do. When I got pushback from my boss, I said, "We've got time, they'll learn more and be better problem-solvers if we allow them to go down the path that isn't going to get them to the right result." I wasn't stupid about it by costing the company lots of money, because I knew, in the long run, we'd be better off as a company if we let employees take the time to work through issues so they could learn.

I attribute my role in my family as the one who stood up to my dad, to prepare me to stand up for my employees; because I cared about their well-being just as much as I cared about the company's success.

6. Challenge Yourself to Change the Family Pattern *for You.*

Before my parents died, I made peace with each of them. I greatly admire that, before my mom died, she wanted to patch up hurts with each of her kids and attended her own therapy. I, along with some of my siblings, attended some of those sessions with her to work through how we were impacted by our family dynamics and the part she had in allowing it.

Over the past 20 years, I have consistently worked at growing as a person (and still do)—not allowing negativity to take me off course from who I want to be. I've learned how to accept and love family members, where there had been strife. I've worked hard at working through the impact of my family dynamics without robbing anyone of his or her dignity, and protecting my own. I've learned how to have honest (and emotional) conversations that have replaced blame with understanding. Being able to listen to what's important to others has given me anappreciation for understanding the motivation behind the choices people make. Everybody approaches situations differently. It doesn't mean they can't change, but I accept people as they are, focus on the positive, and try to bring out the best in people. I stand my ground and don't get wound up in their drama.

To those leaders who don't believe that self-awareness or emotional intelligence benefits their leadership style, and who tend to be on the self-sufficient side of how they handle themselves, my message to them is simple: Understanding the impact of my family dynamics has only enhanced my leadership effectiveness. By being open to personal growth, including learning about my family, I've learned different angles of difficult life events that I never would have thought of had I stayed in my aggressive personality style, closed to growth. Personal growth has enhanced my professional growth.

> *Understanding the impact of my family dynamics has only enhanced my leadership effectiveness.*

I've held myself accountable for changing the only person I can change, and as a result I've changed my family pattern even when some of my family members haven't. I'm still in a relationship with all of my living siblings. Even if we have different opinions, we focus on the relationship more than the differences, and that is a changed pattern!

The Family Factor:
Changing Your Response Changes the System

June's story provides a powerful example of how one person can make a difference by taking responsibility for changing their negative reactive tendencies during conflict—reactive tendencies usually acquired during their childhood. The Family Factor for June manifested itself in the aggressiveness of her leadership style. Conflict management in June's childhood consisted of extreme aggression and brutal anger, and she originally brought that aggression to her workplace. As June progressed in her recovery from alcoholism and came to appreciate the power of emotional intelligence, she initiated a positive ripple effect that changed her family system and the organizational cultures in which she worked.

Using the Emotional Intelligence framework from *Emotional Intelligence 2.0* by Travis Bradberry and Jean Greaves, the following are examples of how June's changed conflict response strengthened her emotional intelligence.

1. Self-awareness

"Your ability to accurately perceive your own emotions in the moment and understand your tendencies across situations."

June first recognized how alcohol became her way of coping with anxiety from years of trauma growing up in a high-conflict, chaotic home environment. She took responsibility to seek out help through her company's EAP program to start on the road to recovery from alcoholism.

Through therapy, June became more aware of the unproductive effect that her anger had on others. Co-workers and employees didn't listen to her or take her seriously. They just saw the anger. June acquired the emotional intelligence skills to avoid overreacting and, instead, to accept that others may have an opinion. And if she disagreed with someone's opinion, she engaged in dialogue and conversation rather than being aggressive with the person.

Her final epiphany, which occurred years after the situation, involved her job with the brutal boss that she had hesitated to leave. June became aware that the reason she had stayed at this job was because it was similar to her family upbringing. Her tendency had been to be comfortable with dysfunction.

Through her own personal growth, June learned that dysfunction, whether caused by the anger of others or by her own overreactions, wasn't acceptable. A childhood of chaos and conflict became an adulthood in which conflict at home and at work was addressed through listening and two-way conversation.

"I realized I was worthy of being treated better than how I was being treated. It was through getting sober and gaining self-awareness in therapy that I got to the root of why I had stayed so long. Bottom line: quality of life wins over materialistic possessions—and I faced the fears of the unknown rather than stay with the chaos and abuse of what was familiar to me."

2. Self-management

"Your ability to use your awareness of your emotions to stay flexible and direct your behavior positively."

As June gained self-awareness of how her behavior impacted others, she developed skills to help transform her reactive tendency of being "overly aggressive" and "bully-my-way-through" to be heard. In addition to her personal work through sobriety and therapy, the leadership development programs she attended through her employer were instrumental in helping her to change her emotional reactions in work situations.

3. Social Awareness

"Your ability to accurately pick up on emotions in other people and understand what is really going on with them."

June's example of how she learned empathy the hard way—when she missed picking up the emotions of one of her employees when his girlfriend's pet died—is a common miss for leaders. Until recent years, the norm has been to keep emotions out of the workplace. Yet as June discovered, having empathy for her employees made her a better leader and in turn led to more productive employees.

Brené Brown's research has validated the need for more leaders "who are committed to courageous, wholehearted leadership and who are self-aware enough to lead from their hearts, rather than unevolved leaders who lead from hurt and fear." June transformed leading from her hurt and fear to leading from her heart.

4. Relationship Management

"Your ability to use your awareness of your own emotions and those of others to manage interactions successfully. This ensures clear communication and effective handling of conflict."

Early on in her recovery, June recognized there wasn't a quick-fix approach to changing her family patterns. She stayed focused on being consistent in changing how she responded to the high emotions of others, without joining their reactivity.

A key skill in relationship management is recognizing that others can have different opinions, wants, and feelings that are the root of conflict, and finding ways to stay connected instead of alienating to resolve conflicts. Easier said than done!

Kathleen K. Wiseman makes the analogy of how to observe the emotions of others, without getting caught up in them, as similar to the view from the bleachers at a football game:

"Picture yourself standing on the sideline at the 50-yard line of a football game, having a close-up appreciation of individual actions and reactions. From that vantage point, you can describe individual characteristics and attributes and make judgments about individual skills and abilities. Alternatively, you can climb to the top of the bleachers and see patterns and forces as groups of individuals act and react to each other over time. Individual characteristics, so important from the 50-yard line, diminish in relation to the broader perspective provided by distance. Broad discernment of patterns provides the viewer with multiple levels of inquiry."

Both with her family and with work relationships, June developed emotional intelligence skills that facilitated her ability to stay connected with others while staying separate from the dysfunction. She made a conscious choice, especially when met with resistance from others, not to revert back to negative, reactive tendencies. June's story shows how one person's growth and development is a catalyst for positive change throughout the family and the organizational system.

References

Bradberry, Travis, and Jean Greaves. *Emotional Intelligence 2.0*. San Diego: Talent Smart, 2009.

Brown, Brené. Dare to Lead: Brave Work. *Tough Conversations. Whole Hearts*. New York: Random House, 2018.

Wiseman, Kathleen K. "Life at Work: The View From the Bleachers." In Ruth Riley Sagar, Managing Editor, Patricia A. Comella, Joyce Bader, Judith S. Ball, and Kathleen K. Wiseman, Editors. *The Emotional Side of Organizations: Applications of Bowen Theory*. Papers Presented at the Georgetown Family Center's Conference on Organizations, April 22-23, 1995. Washington, D.C.: Georgetown Family Center, 1996.

Self-Reflection Questions

1. In what ways do you relate to June's family dynamics?

2. For June, 12-step recovery, therapy, and leadership development were foundational ways she developed emotional intelligence skills. How are you currently developing your emotional intelligence skills?

3. What steps will you take to gain self-awareness in order to interact with co-workers and employees from your heart rather than from hurt and fear?

4. Consider a current relationship in which you're in conflict. How might you see the conflict differently and with a broader perspective of the patterns happening, if you viewed the situation as if from the "bleachers"?

5. If you make a concerted effort to change your conflict pattern, from who do you anticipate getting the most "pushback" in an attempt to get you back to your previous reactive ways of dealing with conflict?

The job of parents is to model. Modeling includes how to be a man or woman; how to relate intimately to another person; how to acknowledge and express emotions; how to fight fairly; how to have physical, emotional and intellectual boundaries; how to communicate; how to cope and survive life's unending problems; how to be self-disciplined; and how to love oneself and another. Shame-based parents cannot do any of these. They simply don't know how.

—John Bradshaw, *Healing the Shame that Binds You*

CHAPTER FOUR

Mike's Story
Breaking The Anger Cycle

Chapter Summary: Even when parents aren't able to model positive conflict management skills, it's never too late to learn how to change patterns of family upbringing and break dysfunctional behaviors. Mike's story reveals his courage and pertinacity to break the family cycle of anger to create better relationships at home—and in the workplace.

Avoiding Conflict to Escape Anger

I grew up in a very authoritarian household. My dad was military, and there was no doubt who was in charge—and take charge he did! He gave orders instead of asking questions. Mom was very compliant and went along to get along. She tended to avoid conflict, even ran from it. I grew up one of four boys. There was always some mischief going on that contributed to my father's anger, which came out through loud voices and eventually, yelling. Gratefully, there was never any physical hitting.

There are two ways to respond to anger: getting angry yourself or staying quiet to avoid the wrath.

As a kid, when things got tense in our family, I responded like my mom by avoiding conflict and adopting the mindset that "things will work out on their own." Other times, I would try to ease the tension by being over-accommodating to others just to keep the peace.

When I think of the impact on the anger cycle and how it has affected my personal life, what strikes me most is the effect it had on my self-confidence. I now see how it affected my desire to play sports; I actually quit sports earlier in my life because I didn't want my dad getting angry at me because I didn't perform as well as he thought I could. As I reflect on other aspects of my life, I now realize that I quit or avoided certain areas of life for the same reason: I didn't want to incur his wrath. How sad. How much of life did I miss because of fear, fear of something that may or may not have happened? I sure hope such fear doesn't rule my daughters' lives.

How My Family Shows Up in My Office

Unfortunately, as an adult, I adopted the angry behavior that was modeled by my parents. This was true in my personal life—I was an angry parent until the events I describe below changed my approach to parenting. And in my professional life, I was also prone to anger and overreaction.

Yet, at the same time, I felt in my professional life—both military and post-military careers—the same impact of the anger cycle on my self-confidence that I experienced as a kid. Sometimes, instead of dealing with a difficult situation, I would try to avoid conflict by ignoring "the elephant in the room."

When I was a young branch chief, having just recently moved to a new base, I had a team of five junior officers who had just completed a major project. One of them was the interim chief while they waited for my arrival.

Within a few weeks, we had significant personality conflicts, which became a problem. At the heart of it, they didn't believe they needed a new boss, as they thought they handled things during their busiest part of the year just fine. Mostly, I failed to acknowledge their work. Yes, I did mention it once, but I should have said it over and over at the appropriate times so they believed me. But I didn't. I also didn't deal with what became a form of insubordination: passive resistance. Based on my upbringing, I avoided addressing conflict at all costs. Big mistake. Had I dealt with it immediately, we could have made it work. But I didn't, and it festered for months until I was promoted and moved to a bigger position in the organization.

Changing the Pattern

Unfortunately, as a parent, my go-to response to conflict and issues was anger. However, I had an epiphany that the way I responded to conflict was not effective. Three distinct incidents were my "wake-up call" to the fact that there was a much easier, more caring, and less stressful way to address conflict. Each of the following three incidents is like a "freeze frame" in my mind—like an instantaneous flashback to the incident to see how others responded to me. All of them have to do with how I parented my children, and they inspired me to make a clear, conscious decision to choose to respond differently from that point on. And I also took the lessons from these incidents into the office.

First Incident

My wife and two daughters were at a friend's house. My friend and I were both in the military, and my wife and his wife were roommates in college and best friends. When their pre-teen son did something stupid and offensive, instead of blowing up and making a scene over it, the dad lovingly but firmly corrected and admonished his son. He called him out, without any emotion, and held his son accountable. The son, realizing he was "busted," came clean, apologized, and moved on. Wow! Can discipline be that easy? Can confrontation be non-confrontational? Yes and YES!

Watching this cut me to the core—I would have had a major meltdown over what his son did, made a huge scene, and been mad at my son for days. But he didn't . . . and it worked. Wow! I changed my behavior immediately after witnessing this.

Lesson Learned: Let love and genuine care be abundantly evident when correcting someone, especially a loved one!

Second Incident

At about the same time, my parents came to visit us. We went to a very formal dinner at the Officer's Club on the Air Force Base where I was stationed. We were all dressed in our Sunday best and our two daughters—who were about four and six at the time—were as cute as they could be in the gorgeous dresses they were wearing.

As we were finishing our long dinner, my daughters became restless and started moving around in their seats. They were not a significant distraction—they were just bored. But the way my dad responded to it was as if they had committed some egregious social faux pas: he quickly lit up.

Immediately—and for the first time—I was transported back in time, and the scene was playing out with me, not my daughters, being admonished to "act my age" by Dad.

I also saw how and why I reacted to my daughters' behaviors—Dad "modeled" for me how to handle "misbehaving children" and I responded exactly as he did, making a big deal about nothing.

Again, on the spot, it was a huge "aha!" moment. I finally understood why I reacted the way I did when my daughters did something. But I also realized that I didn't have to respond that way, just as I had learned a few months earlier when I saw how our friend lovingly corrected his son.

Lesson Learned: Respond/react proportionally to the infraction.

Third Incident

Now it's a few years later from the above incidents. We are living in another state after being transferred yet again.

We were all in the car, and I pulled into a big parking lot so we could go shopping and then get something to eat. As my youngest daughter opened the door, she opened it all the way, smacking it into the light post that was used to illuminate the parking lot. I immediately responded the way I used to—yelling at her, being nasty about it, and fuming.

Later, as my wife was trying to console her, my daughter asked why I parked where I did—I could have avoided the whole situation if I had been a little more thoughtful.

Bam! Ouch! Yes, why didn't I think, why didn't I avoid the entire situation?

Lesson Learned: This was a powerful lesson—leaders think through the situation and try to avoid setting up anyone for failure.

Productive Conflict Management Strategies

1. Ask for Help to Gain Self-Awareness.

After many failed relationships and heart-wrenching moments resulting from not handling conflict well, I went to counseling—to better understand myself, learn how I could get closer to my children, and one day be a caring grandfather. As the saying goes, "Hindsight is 20/20." Through counseling, I came to understand my parents better and to appreciate that they did the best they could based on behaviors that were modeled to them. I have nothing against my parents and I believe that my dad was perhaps the finest model of officership I ever witnessed.

I understand my dad didn't know how to handle conflict other than in an aggressive manner and my mom handled conflict with conformity: "Go along to get along." Neither of them had a role model to teach them to react any differently.

As a youth, Dad grew up in an extraordinarily wealthy family until the depression hit and they lost everything. Dad went from a pampered life to literally trying to learn how to boil water. His parents divorced over the financial crisis at a time when divorce was relatively rare. He graduated from college and had started working when he was drafted into the army in his early 20s. He served in World War II as a mortuary officer in three invasions: Africa, Sicily, and Italy. He never talked about what he went through in the war. Mom was an only child, and her dad was very stern. When they grew up in the 1920s and 1930s, people didn't talk about feelings or disclose personal thoughts. Only on rare occasions would men show emotion or affection.

Though I can't undo the past, nor the times I didn't handle conflict well, counseling helped me make sense of events from my upbringing and forgive myself as I moved past some of my blind spots.

2. Deal with the Elephant in the Room, Immediately.

Unresolved conflict is the elephant in the room. Deal with it immediately. The longer it festers, the harder it is to address and resolve.

Since the incident of the junior officers passively resisting me, I no longer wait to address conflict; I no longer pretend there isn't a problem—I address it head on as quickly as I can. I feel so much better, have fewer sleepless nights, and experience less tension by addressing conflict early.

3. Read for Personal Growth.

I love to read biographies, history, and business management books that have a common theme of how leaders changed or adapted to a difficult situation and prevailed.

One book, in particular, that was very instrumental to me was *Homecoming: Reclaiming and Championing Your Inner Child* by John Bradshaw. From that book, I was convinced that regardless of what happened in my upbringing, I could break the cycle of conflict avoidance and anger. I had a deep desire to change the behaviors that were modeled to me. Reading helps me learn skills and implement changed behaviors for the good. Each day I strive to be a little better than the day before. Reading also helps me apply better behaviors and reaffirms that I can change, just as others have changed as told in the stories I read.

4. Learn Love from Your Faith.

My faith has been fundamental to me in breaking the angry, conflict-avoidance cycle from my family upbringing. It's taken several years for me to connect what I say and do at church on Sunday with what I need to say and do the rest of the time. Sad, but true, and way too typical. But if my faith means anything, it must mean that my default position should be love, and not my life conditioning. I learned that I can choose how I respond. I now choose to be slow to anger but eager to love. In the final analysis, what else is there but love? I hope there are more memories of my love than my rage.

5. Get All the Facts, First and Foremost; Then Respond Proportionally.

In the final analysis, most errors are generally inconsequential. They don't seem that way when an incident happens, but after the dust clears, they aren't as big a deal as we (or my dad) first thought. I have the benefit of time now—some call this "wisdom"—to be able to instantly judge the significance of the error. What I've learned is that very few screw-ups are life-threatening: business will

> *Dad never asked for input . . . Had he asked, he could have avoided conflict from the start, and so can we.*

go on, people will soon forget, and we must dwell on what is important. What's important are relationships. In the final analysis, most of life's meaning comes down to relationships. If that is true, then we must adjust our thoughts and actions and focus on what is really important and strive to restore any broken relationships.

6. Get Input from All Stakeholders Before Beginning a New Project, Policy, Deal, etc.

The expression, "People support the world they help create" is so true. Dad never asked for input, and while he was usually right about most things, there were times he was not. Had he asked, he could have avoided conflict from the start, and so can we. Whether it's preparing our division's input into the company strategic plan, or planning a family vacation, we will be miles ahead if we intentionally seek out input for the documents and actions we will be working on or living out. So why not ask—at the beginning—those individuals on whom we depend, for their input? Even if we already have an idea crafted, we are better served by modeling how we need each other. What a wonderful way to make a lifelong connection with another person: tell them and then show them how we need them.

7. Show Genuine Care and Even Affection to Those That You Lead!

The evidence from studies on employee engagement is consistent: what drives engagement is having immediate bosses who genuinely care about the individuals they supervise (and, supposedly, lead).

Care is spelled, T I M E. Bosses need to take time and Manage by Wandering Around (MBWA) as Tom Peters described in his classic book, *In Search of Excellence*. You can't say you care about your people and not spend time with them on a consistent basis. Just walking (wandering) around the employees every day makes us visible, approachable, and worthy of being called a boss.

8. Follow Dale Carnegie's Advice of "Don't Condemn, Criticize, or Complain."

Alan Mulally followed that advice when he took over as CEO of Ford Motor Corporation. He inherited a lot of conflicts and major problems—the company was literally months away from closing its doors. No one would have blamed him for being nasty and ugly as he struggled to deal with all the problems in front of him. But he chose not to be ugly or to put anyone on the spot. He chose to model true leadership, and he turned the company around. It's an amazing story, one that was predicated on the principle that everyone has worth, so treat everyone with dignity. There's no need to condemn, criticize, or complain if we adopt that principle. Wish I had followed that advice when I was raising my daughters (and so do they . . .).

The Family Factor:
Changing Angry Patterns Takes
Courage, Vulnerability, and Pertinacity

According to Webster's dictionary, courage is defined as "mental or moral strength to venture, persevere, and withstand danger, fear, or difficulty."

Mike's story exhibits the type of courage that is less about facing physical danger, although in some families that might be the case. His courage is the courage to be emotionally vulnerable; the courage to identify and express vulnerable feelings that lurk underneath anger; and the courage that gets to the heart of addressing and ultimately resolving conflict.

In his story, Mike acknowledges with vulnerability the Family Factor that impacted his life—specifically his fear of conflict and disappointing his father. He acknowledges how this fear held him back from taking more risks throughout his life.

Mike's Family Factor is familiar to many men who have learned either through family messages and/or through American culture:

- to be stoic—"showing emotion is a sign of weakness"
- to put forth a "stiff upper lip"
- "real men don't cry"

Especially coming from a military family and serving in the military himself, those messages were modeled and expected of Mike.

In both my counseling and coaching practice, I often hear from men the impact of the above messages that limit their ability to:

- identify vulnerable feelings
- feel vulnerable feelings (without quickly moving to eliminate them)

- listen and be with others when they're expressing vulnerable feelings

In sorting through this dilemma of how to show emotion (other than anger) without feeling less than a man, many of my male clients identified what they were really longing for—approval from their fathers as men, and hearing the words, "I love you."

One father/son session from several years ago in my therapy practice is still vivid in my mind. An adult son said to his father, "I always wanted to know if I was good enough in your eyes. I wanted to hear from you that you loved me." The father paused. After a few minutes passed, with tears in his eyes, he said, "Son, you were always good enough. I always loved you. I didn't know how to say it. I didn't hear those words from my father."

The father and son embraced and both shared tears of appreciation for one another and gratitude for the conversation ... It was a breakthrough to a deeper, more meaningful relationship for both of them.

The father and son embraced and both shared tears of appreciation for one another and gratitude for the conversation that was years in the making. It was a breakthrough to a deeper, more meaningful relationship for both of them.

Although Mike never had this type of vulnerable conversation with his dad, the three incidents he described gave him the motivation and courage to consciously choose to respond to anger differently. He was intentional about learning skills to change how he handled anger that impacted both his personal life and leadership style.

Mike's story is a tribute to the courage and vulnerability required to change family conflict patterns. Through Mike's consistent efforts over time—his pertinacity—it was as if blinders were lifted that revealed how his anger impacted others, both at home and at work. He also gained self-awareness of how the avoidance of directly addressing anger in his family contributed to the elephant in the room—the

Mokita—and impacted Mike's parenting and self-confidence. These events opened the door for Mike to free himself from personal shame and blame towards others, and develop empathy for himself and those around him.

Empathy in Action

In *Dare To Lead,* author Brené Brown refers to five elements of empathy:

1. To see the world as others see it (or perspective taking).

2. To be nonjudgmental.

3. To understand another person's feelings.

4. To communicate your understanding of that person's feelings.

5. Mindfulness (paying attention).

Without realizing it, Mike applied each of the above five elements of empathy to turn around his angry conflict style at home and in the office:

- He gained perspective by seeing the world through his daughters' eyes.

- He stopped judging his children's misbehavior and looked at his own behavior.

- He understood how his anger contributed to his daughters' tears and fears.

- He gained understanding of his parents' upbringing; that upbringing affected how his parents handled emotions and in turn affected him.

- He became mindful—paying attention to the Family Factor effect of anger from one generation to the next.

- He showed how changing one's family conflict pattern of anger can transform—leading from anger and fear to leading with compassion and empathy.

Anger is an emotion that signals that something is at stake, that something is different from what the person who is angry expected. It might be a wish, belief, or unresolved loss that's not been addressed. The good news, as Mike has shared, is that when the underlying emotions of anger are acknowledged, it can be man-aged and transformed. By becoming aware of the vulnerable emotions that are driving your anger, you can make a conscious choice to break the anger cycle in your family, which starts with developing empathy for how your anger impacts those in your personal and work life.

By becoming aware of the vulnerable emotions that are driving your anger, you can make a conscious choice to break the anger cycle in your family . . .

References

Brown, Brené. *Dare to Lead: Brave Work. Tough Conversations. Whole Hearts.* New York: Random House, 2018.

"Courage," Merriam Webster dictionary, accessed December 16, 2019, https://www.merriam-webster.com/dictionary/courage?src=search-dict-box#learn-more

Peters, Thomas J., and Robert H. Waterman, Jr. *In Search of Excellence: Lessons from America's Best-Run Companies.* New York: Harper and Row, 1982.

Self-Reflection Questions

1. How do you tend to handle anger?
   a. yell?
   b. blame others?
   c. hold it inside?
   d. overreact to an incident that's unrelated to what you're really angry about?
   e. other?

2. What were the messages and/or modeling in your family on how to handle anger?

3. In what ways do you handle anger at home or at work? Are they the same or different from what was modeled to you?

4. In applying Brené Brown's five elements of empathy, how does your anger affect those around you?

5. Considering a recent incident when you felt angry, what might be the vulnerable feelings underneath your anger, e.g., fear, embarrassment, grief, insecurity?

Anybody can become angry—that is easy, but to be angry with the right person and to the right degree and at the right time and for the right purpose, and in the right way—that is not within everybody's power and is not easy.

—Aristotle

CHAPTER FIVE

Lee's Story
A History Of Angry Outbursts Inspires Calm And Intentionality

Chapter Summary: Lee is a successful senior leader who learned at a young age how to confront conflict calmly and rationally. Having grown up with a dad who had unpredictable anger outbursts, she learned how to weather the storm, and early on, decided her own leadership style would be storm-free.

An Honorable Man with a Temper

My dad was a good, honorable man, but he had a temper. At times his Italian temper would get the best of him. It wasn't unusual for him to blow up in anger and yell when things didn't go his way. Gratefully, he didn't scream at me, my siblings, or my mom, but we all knew to stay away from him when he started yelling. Now as I look back, the unspoken motto in our family was "this too shall pass"—meaning that within minutes, sometimes a few hours, everything would be fine again.

My siblings and I knew how easily our dad got angry, so we did what we were supposed to do in following the rules and doing well in school. When he was upset with us, he wouldn't yell at us but he would tell us he was disappointed. Disappointing him was something we didn't want to do, which motivated us to do better.

The Messenger

Growing up, I tended to avoid addressing tense situations and learned to let things work out on their own. While I'm the youngest of my siblings, I tended to function like an oldest child in that I would take the initiative to attempt to calm tensions down. It wasn't uncommon that when my older siblings wanted something from Dad, I was the one they sent to ask him. They thought he favored me. I never saw it that way and I believe to this day if they would have asked him for things, he would have given it to them just like he did with me. Unknowingly at the time, this was a skill I was learning that would help me later in life.

How My Family Shows Up in My Office

While there was no one "aha!" moment of how my family shows up in my office, I learned from my father what not to do, and how his anger impacted my mom and us kids. Because of what I saw and experienced, today, I'm intentional in confronting conflict calmly and rationally. I focus on understanding the whole situation in order to make an informed decision. I've made the conscious choice not to exacerbate or make a tense situation worse by having a knee-jerk reaction. I strive to look at both sides and look at all the details involved. That doesn't mean I always look for compromise; I'm not afraid to stir the pot, but somehow, I learned to deal with volatility in others in a calm and analytical manner.

Of course, it doesn't always work out. I'm currently dealing with one of my managers who doesn't realize how her behavior negatively impacts the people she interacts with. She sees herself as right, wanting to move things along, and has called people lazy. I know she has potential as a leader and I've been talking to her about her behavior, but things don't seem to be changing. In order to protect the health of our work culture and negative impact of her behavior on her employees, I'm not afraid to follow through on consequences, starting with a written warning and possibly even termination if she doesn't turn around her abrasive behaviors. That's part of my role as a leader in creating a work environment where everyone feels supported.

Another lesson learned from my upbringing is that, by being the one to go to my father on behalf of my siblings and me, I learned how to present a request with logic and to know the timing of when to ask. From those experiences, I gained skills such as: how to address topics in a forthright manner, and being proactive before a problem arises. My family role has leveraged my career in ways I never would have thought possible, all because I chose to use every opportunity I could to grow and learn.

Productive Conflict Management Strategies

1. Stay Level-headed.

Evaluate your strengths and weaknesses with maturity. Even though my dad had a temper, I learned from those experiences how to handle conflict well and it's helped my career growth as a leader. I didn't want to let him down or him to be disappointed in me, which gave me a healthy respect for authority figures and to make the most of my abilities. It also taught me how, by staying calm, I was better able to present the requests of my siblings with logic and reason. That has been instrumental in my success as a leader.

2. Seek Out a Mentor.

Early in my career, I went to a seasoned leader I respected, looking for someone to run things by. His encouragement and willingness to answer questions I had as a young leader were instrumental in helping me get to where I am today. He later became a colleague, and I'm grateful for the time he took with me that he didn't have to.

3. Be a Lifetime Learner.

As I became more successful, I stayed diligent about putting myself in situations to grow. It was very important to me to do the next right thing. I gained confidence with each success, and as I became more confident, I became more assertive and interacted with people well. I dealt with challenges related to self-esteem and overcame them. Deciding to grow from experiences in my life and my family upbringing, and letting go of issues, has helped me move forward in both my personal and professional lives. I now appreciate the strengths of my father and how he helped to mold the person I am today.

4. Be a Good Listener So You Make Informed, Thoughtful Decisions Instead of Knee-Jerk Reactions.

I knew if I confronted my dad when he was angry, I'd likely get yelled at and make an already tense situation worse. After time passed and my dad cooled down, he was able to be more patient and better able to listen to what my siblings and I wanted. As a leader, when you're under a time crunch and employees' or customers' jobs or lives are at stake, it's difficult to listen to everyone's perspective. You just want to make a decision. Being a good listener allows you to stay objective, weigh the options, and consider the advantages and disadvantages of each option, so you don't make impulsive decisions.

The Family Factor:
Create Psychological Safety
And a "Speak-Up" Work Culture

In 2012, Google did a study called Project Aristotle to determine what factors create a high-performing team. In their quest to answer this question, they looked at 180 teams throughout Google to determine what made some teams get along better than others. They looked at various angles of team members' make-up, such as the gender ratio of each team, the educational backgrounds of team members, and skills.

After two years of analysis, the answer to what factors create high performing teams came down to one primary answer: psychological safety.

The Family Factor for Lee centers around psychological safety, a term coined in 1999 by Harvard Business School professor Amy Edmondson. Edmondson describes "psychological safety" as:

> *a shared belief held by members of a team that the team is safe for interpersonal risk-taking . . . (It instills) a sense of confidence that the team will not embarrass, reject, or punish someone for speaking up. . . It describes a team climate characterized by interpersonal trust and mutual respect in which people are comfortable being themselves.*

When Lee's dad would have angry outbursts, Lee, her siblings, and her mom experienced the opposite of psychological safety. Instead of growing up with the confidence that everyone in the family could have a say, they gauged her dad's mood as to if, and when, to speak up. As a leader, Lee vowed to create psychological safety for her team. As she stated:

> *I learned from my father what not to do and how his anger impacted my mom and us kids. Because of what I saw and experienced, today I'm intentional in confronting conflict calmly and rationally.*

When I coach leaders to turn around abrasive behavior, part of the coaching process is doing 360-degree interviews with employees and co-workers to identify what the leader does that creates negative perceptions of their leadership style. In other words, what behaviors distract from psychological safety.

More often than not, abrasive leaders are genuinely unaware of how they come across to others—specifically, how their behavior impacts employees' comfort level about speaking up with ideas and questions, and most importantly, admitting mistakes.

Common examples of what employees say about the impact of a leader's abrasive behavior are:

- *I can tell by the way he walks in the office what kind of mood he's in and whether to speak to him or avoid him.*

- *Her mood can go from zero to ten in a matter of seconds.*

- *His moods fluctuate depending on who he's talking to. If they're not one of his favorites, people are afraid to approach him for fear of being yelled at, especially in front of other people.*

- *When things aren't going her way, she'll raise her voice and get in people's personal space. She never actually touches you, but you know to get out of her way.*

Just like a parent's mood impacts children, so does a boss's mood impact employees.

As with the abrasive leader, it appears that Lee's dad was not aware of how his anger impacted the family.

Perhaps like Lee, you also learned in your upbringing how to navigate being around people with unpredictable moods, by being aware of when to bring up certain topics. Or, perhaps, you relate to Lee's siblings and avoid interacting with certain co-workers, employees, or bosses for fear of being yelled at.

The Impact of NOT Speaking Up

A study of 1700 healthcare employees revealed that 90 percent wouldn't speak up in the face of poor practice and bad behavior, even in life-and-death situations. That's an astounding percentage! Why are people, who are supposed to be in the profession of helping their patients get well and ensure safety when people are ill, not

... 90 percent wouldn't speak up in the face of poor practice and bad behavior, even in life-and-death situations.

speaking up even when they see inappropriate behavior that could harm others?

According to nurse bullying expert Renee Thompson, there are three primary reasons: fear, futility, and lack of accountability.

1. **Fear.** People fear the consequences of how people will respond—such as retaliation—if their behavior is challenged. Will this person find a way to get back at me? Another fear is, if I raise this concern, will this person downplay the incident and turn the tables on me as if I'm the one with the problem?
2. **Futility.** If people do speak up to their leader, nothing is done to rectify the situation. They become complacent because they don't see anything happening to the person exhibiting the bad behavior, so they feel a sense of futility.
3. **Lack of accountability.** People think it's the leader's responsibility to take action. Many employees don't see it as their job to speak up or get involved.

Thompson's prescription to eradicate bullying and incivility in healthcare is to make the conscious choice to take action in the face of disruptive behavior.

What you can do . . .

If you relate to Lee's dad and have a tendency towards anger outbursts and unpredictable moods, be willing to identify what's driving your anger and turn around your behavior.

- **Here's why:** One of the best ways you can unleash the individual and collective talent of your employees is by creating a psychologically safe work environment. Not only will your employees be more likely to share information, contribute ideas, and report mistakes, neuroscience shows that they will be more innovative and creative, which leads to greater bottom-line results.

If you relate to Lee's siblings, and tend to be a conflict avoider, be willing to learn skills to address conflict productively and speak up when you see disruptive behavior.

- **Here's why:** Your input is valuable. Period. Now more than ever, with increasing demands and the fast pace of the work world, everyone's input is needed. Especially in situations when disruptive behavior, such as bullying and incivility, exists.

If you relate to Lee, and you are already addressing disruptive behavior, celebrate your courage! Keep modeling productive conflict management skills, including the timing of when to speak up and what to say.

- **Here's why:** Whether you are a leader in title or a leader of yourself, you are a trailblazer in modeling the path out of work cultures that condone silence and tolerate the status quo of "it's not my job," or "that's just the way it is around here."

References

Duhigg, Charles. "What Google Learned from its Quest to Build the Perfect Team." *New York Times Magazine.* February 25, 2016.

Edmondson, Amy. *The Fearless Organization: Creating Psychological Safety in the Workplace for Learning, Innovation, and Growth.* New York: John Wiley, 2018.

Maxfield, David, Grenny, Joseph Grenny, Ron McMillan, Kerry Patterson, and Al Switzler. *Silence Kills: The Seven Crucial Conversations in Healthcare.* Provo, UT: Vital Smarts, 2005.

Thompson, Renee. "Three Tips to Speak Up When Bad Behavior Happens." https://www.youtube.com/watch?v=FjURd-J5fGs. Accessed December 16, 2019.

Self-Reflection Questions

1. When it comes to speaking up and addressing poor behavior in the workplace (i.e., incivility or bullying), who do you relate to in this chapter more? Lee who spoke up or her siblings who avoided the conflict? How?

2. If you could put yourself in the shoes of Lee's dad, or someone in your work setting who leans towards angry outbursts, how could you see them through the eyes of compassion to understand what's driving their anger?

3. In reflecting on your family upbringing, what did people in the family do when someone was angry? How did anger impact you?

4. Who in your family might you have a conversation with to better understand how conflict was handled in your upbringing—with the intent to understand what was driving anger?

5. Which of Lee's Productive Conflict Management Strategies (or one of your own) would help you to contribute to psychological safety in your work setting?

    a. Speak up when you make a mistake?

    b. Speak up when you see bullying behavior in a co-worker?

    c. Speak up in meetings with your ideas that might rock the boat of status quo?

You may not control all the events that happen to you,
but you can decide not to be reduced by them.

—Maya Angelo

CHAPTER SIX

Regina's Story
Overcoming Being Undervalued And Underestimated

Chapter Summary: Regina was raised in an environment of loving parents and expectations. She was taught to be someone others could rely on. Despite how responsible, intelligent, and capable she was, her father undervalued her capabilities. Later in her career, men in the workplace also undervalued her capabilities. Instead of engaging in conflict or carrying resentments, Regina let her GPA, credentials, and career accomplishments speak for themselves. Her story reveals how she didn't allow her family dynamics—which included the loss of her mom at age 12, and later, the resistance of her father to her career as an attorney—nor the prejudices she encountered as a black, female attorney to hold her back from career successes.

Growing Up as the Responsible Child

All of my life, I've been more serious and never rambunctious or challenging toward my parents. My brother entered life bubbly, playful, and always needing to be supervised. Even though my father demonstrated and expected leadership from my brother and me, my brother's childhood was built more on playfulness, while mine was based on taking care of business. My parents knew I could be counted on in any situation.

My parents always modeled responsibility and were serious about life. Before my parents married, my dad had prepared himself to be a better parent than his parents had been. Starting when he was a child, growing up in the South in poor living conditions, he didn't allow his living conditions to dampen his spirits for a better life. He set goals for himself early in life. When he met and married my mom and had children, he fulfilled all the things he prepared himself for as a young man. He was a "step-up" dad, meaning a dad who understood what it meant to be a loving, responsible father.

My mom was always nurturing. She started to read to me daily when I was only three months old. She also showered my brother and me with lots of love. Mother had a caring impact on people and influenced who they became. This included the children at our church, my dad, my brother, and me. And she never expressed resentment for any of the challenges she encountered in life, including the complications from diabetes that eventually took her life.

A Family Life Without Conflict

Conflict in my upbringing was extremely rare. I have only two memories of seeing my parents argue, and both of the incidents were short-lived. My first recollection was walking in on my parents, who were having a disagreement over something. They were outside hanging clothes on the line and having a discussion that was rather heated. Of course, I had no idea what they were talking about, but as soon as they knew I came outside, they stopped and immediately changed the subject. I was like, "Whoa! What's happening here . . . what was that?" They quickly calmed the discussion and assured me that everything was okay. I was probably around 10 years old.

A second incident happened during a family vacation when I was about 11 years old. Part of the reason I remember it is because it was caught on videotape. My parents were again having a "discussion" for lack of a better word, and my mother just shook her head at my father while saying his name, followed by "you're being ridiculous." It's so funny to look back at it now and wonder: what did he say or do?

Those are the only two incidents I can remember from my childhood of conflict between my parents, and both were at a very low level. My parents were married for 21 years so they had to have conflict over the years, every couple does, and discord is in every family. All I can say is, it was pretty well hidden from me.

The Loss of Mom

When I was 12 years old, my mom died. Her death was devastating for all of us. My dad tried to hide his grief. He felt the pressure of being both a mother and father to my brother and me, and he remarried very quickly because he had two children to raise.

His short life with my mother was helpful in preparing him to raise my brother and me alone. She gave Dad the drive to not let life tear him down. During his marriage to my mom, he learned to love, see the best rather than the worst in people, become a giver not a taker, and love his wife. He credits my mom with helping him to be the best man he could be.

Mom's Encouragement, Dad's Resistance

Before my mom died, she wrote me letters. The letters kept me connected to her while she was in the hospital. They were sweet and endearing. She was a great encourager to me, and she saw potential in my dream to become a lawyer.

It took my dad a while to embrace my dream. He wanted me to be an engineer. He was a union official and negotiated contracts, interacting with corporate, and he knew there was a lot of pressure in being an attorney. He saw people's health fail due to the stresses they faced. He wanted me to have more of a low-stress job so I wouldn't have the "pressure cooker" life of an attorney, especially as a litigator. Dad also wanted me to have job security like he did. His company employed lots of engineers and he saw engineering as a reliable job for me that would also provide excellent pay. Because of his connections, he figured he could help me find a good engineering job if I stayed in the Midwest.

Before Mom died, Dad had promised her that both my brother and I would attend college. When it came time to go to college, I stood up to my dad and let him know that either I go to college and become a lawyer, or I'm not going. He finally agreed to my wishes, then worked on my brother to become an engineer.

Proving Myself to Dad

It felt like I always had to prove myself to my dad and show him that I was capable. As we were growing up, he would talk about my brother being smart, but he never called me smart. For some reason Dad had a hard time acknowledging my successes. It's almost laughable now when I think about it. After I "proved" myself to him in college, he would give me whatever I wanted, like his credit card. Now that I think about it, maybe it was guilt that stopped him from encouraging me earlier. Let's just say initially, he didn't put roadblocks in my way but he sure wasn't a cheerleader for me going to college to become a lawyer.

Until I went away to college and came back home, Dad was on pins and needles. He was concerned about what I was doing and who I was with. I understand now, in retrospect, that he didn't want me to have a boyfriend or a car for fear of something happening to me that would take me off track from my goals. I finished my first semester with a boyfriend and a 3.79 GPA, and graduated summa cum laude. He was floored. And then when I graduated with honors from law school, he fell out of his chair! He even bought me a car! I finally proved to him that I could make good grades.

I don't have any bad feelings toward my dad. He's from Tennessee, but he acts as if he's from Missouri—the "Show Me" state—and he wants to see something before he believes it. His saying is, "You can say this and you can say that, but the proof is in the pudding."

How My Family Shows Up in My Office

Growing up, I had to prove to my dad that I could become a lawyer. In various jobs throughout my career, I remember having to prove myself to men, and they were white men at that. I've had a lot of "firsts" in my career, like helping to start a new satellite office for a national law firm, where I was the only woman and the only person of color. There have been times when racially inappropriate comments

Those struggles were stepping stones . . . I use those experiences to propel myself in my passion for diversity in the workplace, because I know what it's like to be questioned about whether I'm capable.

were said and my competency was questioned, even though the law partners recruited me and I was sought after because of my resume, credentials, and having graduated with honors.

Today, as I have transitioned to the roles of vice president and general counsel, those events are water under the bridge to me. I don't hold any resentment toward those who didn't believe in me, including my father. I have a job I enjoy and I am appreciated. Those struggles were stepping stones to get me to where I am today. I use those experiences to propel myself in my passion for diversity in the workplace because I know what it's like to be questioned about whether I'm capable—first by my father, which came from his wanting to protect me from the pressures of being a lawyer, and then in various work situations because of my skin color.

Another way that my family background shows up in my office is that I've always been the "go-to" person without even realizing it. When something needs to get done, people come to me. They know I have an eye for detail and consistency. Today at work I'm known as the "It" girl; this was also the role I had in my family growing up.

My Two-Tiered Response to Conflict

Growing up in a house without conflict didn't give me the skills I needed to confront conflict directly, and speak up in the moment. It wasn't until my late teen years, when the decision was being made about my going to college, that I realized the importance of standing up to my dad. That's why today I deal with conflict with a combination of avoidance, while still calling conflict out for what it is. That's what I call my two-tiered response. I'm usually pretty perceptive about recognizing when there's an issue or a concern, figuring out how to work through it and make things happen for the good. At the same time, although I'm willing to stand up for myself, I still try to avoid conflict if at all possible. If I see an issue potentially coming to a head, I try to derail it or realign it somehow. I strive to be proactive rather than reactive.

It's funny, I'm a lawyer, but I don't like conflict. I think that's why I'm in the role I am today as general counsel for a non-profit organization: to get away from the intense conflict that lawyers often deal with. When I was in private practice right out of law school and had to go to court and argue with people, that just wasn't me. I remember one of my most profound memories from practicing law. I witnessed two lawyers having a fistfight in the courthouse. That just blew my mind on how things could escalate to that point!

How Strong Women Role Models Pushed Me Forward

Besides my mother, the most influential woman in my life was my godmother, Laura. She's been the closest mother figure to me since my mother died. Of anybody that has been in my life, she reminds me the most of my mom. If I want female advice, I call her.

My earliest memories of wanting to be a lawyer go back to sixth grade when our class watched the Martin Luther King, Jr. documentary. We watched it at school for over a week and had to write papers about it. I couldn't wait to go home and talk to my parents about it! Then in the eighth grade, our class went to Washington, D.C. and I got to see the Constitution, the Bill of Rights—all of these things I had studied in school. When I saw them in person, it just became real to me. There was a passion for social justice issues and history that was stirred up in me that I couldn't explain.

This stirring crystallized into a professional goal, thanks to three strong, successful women lawyers that I was lucky to meet when I was young:

1) Gail. Between my class trip to D.C. and my mom dying, Mom arranged for me to meet one of her childhood friends, Gail, who was an attorney. My mom told her I had just gone to Washington, D.C. and apparently she had already told Gail that I wanted to become a lawyer when I grew up. When Gail visited from New York a short time later, she took me to a courthouse and then to lunch.

We sat in the back of the courtroom during a trial. To this day, I don't remember what she said to me, but I can remember vividly being with her. To meet someone who was doing what I wanted to do and watching the way she handled herself as a professional made it a day I'll never forget!

2) Catherine. Catherine was the first female president of my father's union. Both of my parents had worked for a major automotive manufacturer and my dad was very active in the union. Catherine and my dad would go to blows with each other and I remember I always respected her, thinking, "How does this woman hang with these men?" Then I learned she had a law degree! Bingo!

Catherine went to law school while she was wrestling with all these union issues. Her law degree gave her the skill set to negotiate major collective bargaining agreements and contracts on behalf of the union. My dad would take me to meetings with him and I watched what was happening as they were negotiating contracts. I didn't understand what was happening at the time because I was very young, coloring or playing with my paper dolls, but I was taking it all in!

3) Patricia. Later in my teen years, when my father finally accepted that either I was going to college to become a lawyer or not going at all, Dad—with

Catherine's help—arranged for me to meet Patricia, a lawyer from General Motors who was a black woman.

I don't remember the details of meeting Patricia, but again I remember how I felt. I was in awe of how professional she was—she had a suit on, long pretty hair, and a briefcase. She just looked so together and I thought, "I want to be like that." Patricia left a lasting impression on me. I give my dad and Catherine credit for arranging for me to meet her.

From these three women lawyers—two of them, Gail and Patricia, black—I set my sights on having an in-house attorney career rather than private practice. I saw it as a path to have more lifestyle balance. I wanted to be able to take family vacations and not have a nanny raise my kids. It was so cool to meet women who were already doing what I wanted to do.

An Executive Coach Is Still Helping Me to Keep Moving Forward

The example and support of my parents and my godmother, and the inspiration of the female attorneys, continue to give me strength in dealing with the issues I face today as a high-level black, female attorney. In addition, I've worked with an executive coach for the past five years who's taught me when it's necessary to stand up and be more assertive, as well as provide direction for my own professional development and achievement. Without Donna's coaching, I would be less direct, which is my default. She's been a great encourager to me for addressing issues I would rather avoid.

I enlisted Donna's help initially after watching people in my field that I respected retain coaches to gain direction for their own careers. She's a "recovering lawyer" herself and she understands the challenges of our field. I also participate in coaching because as the saying goes, "It's lonely at the top." I don't have many people that I can confide in and talk to because of the confidential nature of my work. Having a coach to help me navigate through complicated issues has been invaluable. For example, I started working with Donna when I was under 40 years old and the first African-American woman general counsel in a predominately white institution. From the outset, she had a way of asking me questions that have helped me manage some political issues, and guided me to my own answers without telling me what to do. It's been in the context of answering her coaching questions out loud that I realized I have the answers within me, and as a result, have changed my tendency to avoid difficult topics.

Productive Conflict Management Strategies

1. Set Boundaries.

Because I'm the "It" girl at work, I've ended up with too many things on my to-do list because people know "if you want it done, give it to Regina." As the saying goes, "If you want something done, give it to a busy person."

2. Stand Firm in Your Convictions.

While I didn't realize it at the time, when I stood my ground with my dad, it was a defining moment that would help me the rest of my life. Not only did it help me to fulfill my promise to my mom and go to college to become a lawyer, it taught me the importance of taking a stand for what's important to me. Although I knew my dad loved me and was trying to protect me, I became my own person when I stood up to him, and he eventually saw I was more capable than he realized.

3. Always Stand Up and Be Counted.

Related to above, be a voice at the table of high-level management discussions for your race and gender. Voice your concerns or questions. Diversity serves a purpose in helping us see problems or situations from different perspectives. Use your voice to effect change.

4. Have Conversations with People Who Are Where You Want to Be.

Meeting Catherine, Gail, and Patricia was instrumental in propelling me toward my career as a lawyer. Having a positive female role model like my godmother, after my mother passed, has helped me to become the woman I am today.

5. Use a Coach.

In addition to my coach helping me handle conflict more effectively, coaching has also helped me say "no" more often. Donna has helped me to be more selective in my commitments, so I find more personal satisfaction in my work, and don't burn myself out or become resentful.

6. Give Back Through Volunteering.

Beyond your day-to-day job, be involved in your community to make a difference about what's important to you, while using your skill set. Even though my direct professional role today doesn't involve social justice, I've been very active with the local minority bar associations and local churches in an effort to help ex-felons have their voting rights restored. Through this initiative, I've broadened my horizons and learned about criminal law. When you give back through volunteering, not only does it help your community, you also meet different types of people and learn in ways you wouldn't have if you didn't get involved. I believe that the more well-rounded you are as a person, the more open-minded you are likely to be in conflict situations.

The Family Factor:
Speak Up About What's Important to You

For Regina, the Family Factor is her early history of being consistently undervalued by her father. In dealing with her father, Regina developed the resilience to overcome skepticism and lack of respect—a resilience that would be vital to her success when she encountered similar skepticism and lack of respect from male lawyers, especially white men.

A defining moment in Regina's life was when she spoke up to her father and said, "Either I go to college to become a lawyer or I'm not going." What Regina did in that moment became a pivotal shift from being a conflict avoider at any cost to speaking up for what was important to her. In essence she said, "Dad, I love you, *and* I'm going to be my own person whether you like it or not." It was a defining moment that proved she was capable of thinking for herself and making decisions for her life.

It's understandable her father wanted what he thought was best for his daughter. That's what all loving parents want. In his work life, he saw how challenging a lawyer's work was and wanted to protect her from a stressful life ahead. What her father seemed to underestimate were her capabilities, and the depth of conviction Regina had to fulfill her promise to her mother before she died, even if her father didn't agree with her decision.

A key developmental milestone of maturity in psychology terms is called "differentiation." A term coined in the 1950s by the father of Family Therapy, Murray Bowen, differentiation means:

- *identifying* what you think and feel about a given situation and staying true in your heart to what's important to you, when faced with others who disagree

- *speaking up* for what you want, while tolerating the pushback from others who see things differently than you do

- if and when setting boundaries, *listening* in order to understand others' points of view, without giving up on what's important to you

Differentiation doesn't mean you always get your way. It doesn't mean "my way or the highway." It does mean staying calm and connected with others, so each person can express his or her perspective in order to work through differences. Ideally, the relationship gets healthier and stronger as a result of everyone involved being direct, honest, and respectful of one another—especially if others think differently than you. Regina's relationship with her father became healthier when she clearly defined what she wanted, even when it wasn't what her father wanted for her.

Differentiation in the Workplace

Being able to differentiate yourself applies to the workplace as much as it does to your personal life, especially during conflict. Whether you are offering a different perspective during a staff meeting, addressing a problem with your boss, or asking for buy-in from your board of directors, being grounded in self-differentiation will empower you to take risks and create the conditions of collaboration and teamwork.

Becoming self-differentiated is not a "one-and-done" experience. It takes ongoing intentionality, and a conscious choice of being your own person, and expressing your feelings, wants, and wishes, especially when others attempt to pressure you to conform to their way of thinking. Sometimes differentiation becomes messy when you speak up about what *you* want, and others threaten to end the relationship or become angry if you don't do what *they* want. Those are the times when exercising pertinacity by staying calm, steady, and clear about your boundaries, while also listening to others' points of view, will increase your credibility and lead to win-win solutions. Also, keep in mind hearing and validating other people's points of view isn't the same as agreeing with them.

Here are three ways Regina "differentiated" herself in her family that she also applied to the workplace:

1. Know what's important to you. When you face conflict in your personal or professional life, know in advance why the situation is important to you. Get clarity about your thoughts, feelings, and desires so you're unwavering when others push back. Helen Keller said, "The only thing worse than being blind is having sight but no vision." Regina knew she wanted to become a lawyer since she was in sixth grade. She fulfilled her vision of what she wanted as her career choice and wasn't blinded by what her father wanted.

2. Gain self-awareness. You may have clarity about what you want, but lack the skills to make your dream a reality. Regina recognized that her default conflict pattern was avoidance. She knew she wouldn't be a good litigator because she didn't like conflict and therefore chose another area of law to practice in. Even though she got out of litigation, she recognized that if she wanted to excel as a high-level black attorney, she needed to be more assertive and speak up for herself no matter what field of law she practiced in. As a result, she enlisted the support of a leadership coach to improve her interpersonal skills so she could become more assertive and change her tendency to avoid difficult topics.

3. Let your actions speak louder than words. As a black, female lawyer, Regina faced racially inappropriate comments and her competency was questioned. Diversity expert Amy C. Waninger refers to such inappropriate comments as "interpersonal papercuts." These are "the verbal jabs and harmful assumptions, derisive in nature, that are rooted in ignorance, obliviousness, or outright hostility." Waninger states that these interpersonal papercut behaviors are micro-aggressions, "like emotional papercuts that we inflict upon one another, often without realizing it . . . but these seemingly small indignities have a big impact over time." They lead, says Waninger, to "death by a thousand cuts." They may not be noticed initially, yet over time, hurt.

The way Regina has handled the interpersonal papercuts early in her career with her law partners is similar to how she handled her father questioning whether she could make it through college and law school: "the proof is in the pudding." It wasn't until her first year of college when she got a high GPA that her father believed in her potential. Without having an emotional reaction to her law partners, she used the string of interpersonal papercuts as another motivator to let her competency and character be the "proof in the pudding" at work.

One of the hardest things to do in addressing and resolving conflict (and interpersonal papercuts) is to stick with the issue at hand when your fight or flight response kicks in. When emotionally triggered, the natural tendency is to either become defensive or surrender to restore harmony, or walk away. Drawing on your pertinacity to stick with difficult conversations with self-differentiation says, "I care about you, I want to understand where you're coming from; even if we have different perspectives, let's work this out."

It's important to note that there are circumstances when continuing the conversation may be fruitless. In this case, differentiation calls for not forcing the outcome you want and allowing natural consequences to occur. Again, Regina let her skills as an attorney silence the naysayers.

When your boss, co-workers, or employees doubt your capabilities—or worse yet, if your character, race, gender, or sexuality is attacked—sometimes the most differentiated mindset is to "Keep Calm and Carry On," allowing your actions to speak louder than your words. In no way is this response intended to minimize the impact of interpersonal papercuts. Rather, the intent is to determine what your mindset will be when you face them.

We're all very familiar with the World War II poster "Keep Calm and Carry On." What you may not know is that this poster was never actually released during World War II. When Britain was facing the threat of Germany invading the country, three posters with a "stand firm" message were to be distributed to the British people as a message from the King to assure them that everything possible was being done to defend the nation.

Two of the three posters—**"Your Courage, Your Cheerfulness, Your Resolution Will Bring Us Victory"** and **"Freedom Is In Peril: Defend It With All Your Might"**—were displayed in window shops and railway platforms.

But the third poster, which stated **"Keep Calm and Carry On,"** was held in reserve as it was intended to be used only in times of crisis or invasion. That's how potent this mindset of staying calm and letting actions display your pertinacity can be. The idea was to urge the people of England to stay calm and go about their business as much as they could in this time of war, even as the threat of bombs falling on their city hung heavy in the air. The poster was never officially issued until some 50 years later, when a rare copy was discovered in a box of old books purchased at auction by bookstore owners in Alnwick, England. The phrase "Keep Calm and Carry On" is now seen everywhere (and adapted humorously in many ways). But long before it became popular, Regina was following its advice. In some way, bombs—in the form of questions about her competence and skills, if not outright bias and racism—have been falling around her throughout her career; but she goes about her business, and mostly lets her success answer the critics.

When facing conflict, speak up about what's important to you but let your actions do most of the talking—and always keep calm in the process.

References

The Couple's Institute. Online training for "The Developmental Model of Couples Therapy: Integrating Attachment, Differentiation, and Neuroscience." Accessed December 22, 2019.

Waninger, Amy C. Network Beyond Bias: *Making Diversity a Competitive Advantage For Your Career*, McCordsville, INL Lead at Any Level LLC, 2018.

Self-Reflection Questions

1. When you face conflict, how might the situation improve if you first determine what's important to you about the issue before you respond?

2. Review the definition of differentiation. On a scale of 1–10 with 10 being the highest, how would you rate yourself as being "differentiated" during conflict at work?

3. What is one behavior you're willing to implement in order to improve your level of differentiation?

4. Regina describes avoiding conflict if possible, but not at all costs. If you were to "stand up and be counted" on a particular work issue that you've been avoiding, what stand would you take?

5. How would your behavior be different at work if you showed more "self-differentiation" and focused more on changing yourself than focusing on how others need to change?

I think the first step is to understand that forgiveness does not exonerate the perpetrator. Forgiveness liberates the victim. It's a gift you give yourself.

—T.D. Jakes

CHAPTER SEVEN

Will's Story
The Power Of Forgiveness In The Workplace

Chapter Summary: Letting go of bitterness over other's wrongdoing, and forgiving them, is unnatural. It's easier said than done, yet possible. Such was the case with Will. Will's story represents the power of forgiveness as a primary productive conflict strategy and solution to changing the pattern of how to respond to broken trust. Self-awareness of how his own judgmental response to conflict was prolonging the conflict also contributed to changing his conflict management style.

Growing Up with Calm Unpredictability

I grew up in a small Midwestern community where my dad owned a construction company. From his early years as a Marine, Dad learned to be highly disciplined. He was a very calm, composed, and patient man. He had a very high tolerance for drama and high-maintenance people, including a perfect blend of patience and understanding while still being firm. Even when he got angry, he was in control and never compromised his values. He's been my role model, and someone who is an ideal leader.

My mom on the other hand, had a fiery temper and her moods were highly unpredictable. Growing up, I was often embarrassed by my mother's behavior. In addition to multiple broken promises to me, her behavior with my friends and friends' parents put me in a bad light. For example, if she didn't think I was being treated fairly by one of my friends, it wasn't unusual for her to run to my defense and have a shouting match with my friend's mother. I can still see my mom standing on the curb with her left hand on her hip, her right hand flying through the air yelling at my friend's mom about what her kid did to me. Both women would be standing on their side of the street yelling at each other. Those types of incidents happened often and probably contributed to my being bullied in school. I had very little trust in my mother's ability to handle situations appropriately.

Dad did everything he could to protect me from Mom's angry outbursts, especially when she would become so agitated she would throw things. Dad never raised his voice or showed any kind of disrespect to her regardless of how she treated him . . . or me.

Eventually, my parents divorced when I was in junior high school, and my dad got full custody of me. Mom made attempts to stay in touch and made promises to see me or bring me things, but she rarely followed through. I learned not to believe or trust her.

Besides my mother, there was another person who abandoned me as a kid and contributed to my building protective walls around myself. When I was a kid, Dad hired a family member into his construction business who embezzled from him. As a result, my dad lost his very successful, longstanding company. Everything was gone. My dad could have sent this person to jail for at least 30 years, if not longer. He chose not to press charges in order for this person to find work elsewhere and still be able to provide for his family. My dad let the wrongdoing go, found another career and re-established himself, all for the sake of our extended family.

My dad was never bitter; he said, "Bitterness doesn't do anybody any good. If I choose to be bitter, it's only going to harm me—not [this family member]. I don't want to spend the rest of my life being bitter." In contrast, I had another extended family member who made poor financial decisions and lost everything. Unlike my dad, this second family member lived and died with the anger and bitterness still in him.

Dad made the choice to see the loss of his business as temporary; he said, "I'll recover from this—this is only temporary." The family member, on the other hand, had to live permanently with his decision to embezzle from Dad. Dad's perspective on being cheated and losing everything he'd worked so hard for has always stuck with me. He's always concerned about others and sees the best in everyone.

How My Family Shows Up in My Office

I was never one to be afraid of conflict and I don't avoid it. It's not like I look for it, but when it happens, I like to address the problem upfront and find a resolution. What's changed over the years is the way I handle conflict.

I have learned the hard way that when conflict isn't resolved in a manner that will salvage the relationship, both of us end up carrying the emotional luggage with us wherever we go.

Before I gained the awareness that I was dealing with conflict ineffectively, I tended to blame others, pointing out what others did wrong, and tried to control the situation. This only led to more conflict and defensiveness from whomever I was in disagreement with.

A big part of the problem was my lack of trust, which grew out of my relationship with my mom.

I have learned the hard way that when conflict isn't resolved in a manner that will salvage the relationship, both of us end up carrying the emotional luggage with us wherever we go.

So today I run my business on the principal of trust. Even though my dad gave me stability, structure, and guidance, the lack of trust from my mom was predominant in my upbringing. Because of the experiences with my mom, I use that experience to propel me to be a trustworthy person and business leader. I make a conscious effort to ask questions to understand where the other person is coming from and learn from the situation to prevent it from happening again. And for those who have betrayed my trust, I learned to forgive.

Early in my career I met with a prospective client who had been burned by one of my competitors; he was understandably skeptical that I would do the same thing. I don't know where I got this but my immediate response was, "Give me 10 percent of your trust and I'll work my butt off to earn the other 90 percent," and he said, "You have a deal." Trust has been a key driver of my business.

That said, when people don't do what they say they'll do, it hits my trust button. If I'm not aware of how I manage my reaction, I can still revert back to my default response of anger. I can usually contain the anger with my clients. It's when a vendor I work with doesn't keep their word that really triggers me. Now I recognize the anger stems from my experiences as a kid when my mom didn't follow through on her commitments. I'm conscious about monitoring my reaction when people don't follow through, so I don't overreact.

> *. . . the anger stems from my experiences as a kid when my mom didn't follow through on her commitments. I'm conscious about monitoring my reaction when people don't follow through so I don't overreact.*

Another way my family background has impacted how I work is my dad's model of making people the number one priority in his business, and of building relationships; this attitude shows up in my office every day. My closing ratio in my business is extremely high because I choose to incorporate my dad's example of the value of hard work and putting people first into how I run my business. He taught me, "It's not about me; it's about serving them . . . my clients."

That saying also relates to why my dad didn't press charges against the family member who embezzled from him. He knew in the long run that if this family member couldn't work, he wouldn't have been able to provide for his wife and kids. Dad was thinking about the impact on this man's family being worse if their husband and father were in jail. His example of putting people first has really stuck with me.

Events that Impacted the Changing of My Conflict Pattern

The ineffective way I originally dealt with conflict—rooted in a lack of trust stemming from my childhood—came to light for me over a period of time and in a variety of ways. I've always been open to growth and personal development, to be better than I was the day before. Below are six pivotal turning points, the first of which occurred when I was a sophomore in college, and on which I still rely on today.

1. Forgiveness of my mother.

When I was a sophomore in college, my mother was diagnosed with early Alzheimer's. At that point I knew I had a choice to make: to either hold onto my bitterness over her behavior through the years and how she wasn't there for me growing up, and feeling sorry for

I made the conscious choice to release the grudge I had towards her and treat her with compassion.

myself, or dealing with it. I've always been the type of person who chose the latter, and that's what I did.

I became my mother's guardian after she was diagnosed with Alzheimer's. I made the conscious choice to release the grudge I had towards her and treat her with compassion.

2. Relationship with my daughter.

My daughter and I are very much alike. We both like to be in control, and as she got into her teen years, we were arguing a lot. Both of us were telling the other what the other was doing wrong and why we were right. A turning point in our relationship came during an escalated argument; suddenly I realized that as the dad, I've got to cool this down.

I thought to myself, as the adult I need to be the one to say, "Let's take a break, regroup in 15 minutes to take the edge off, think about how we want to approach our differences, and continue the conversation." Since I took that initiative, our relationship improved gradually to the point where now, almost two years later, we get along great.

From that experience with my daughter, I realized how much I was contributing to the angst between us. As her dad and the adult, I wanted to do better. Instead of fighting for control and pointing out her wrongdoing, I started asking more questions and intentionally listening to what she was saying, and checking out what I heard to make sure I understood her.

I also was intentional about listening without correcting her, especially if I saw things differently—while also becoming aware of conveying through my body language that I was open to what she had to say.

This combination of asking her questions, being a better listener, and showing my sincerity through my body language were huge game changers that improved our relationship. I became conscious of how I handled our conflict so she didn't feel hurt afterwards.

Something I wish could have happened between my mother and me.

3. Review of personality profile in grad school.

The third turning point of changing my conflict pattern from controlling to less reactive was when I was in grad school earning a master's in Leadership and

Organizational Development. As part of the program we each took an in-depth personality profile. After reading that, and sharing with my cohort events from my life, I realized there was a better way than my own.

It was a humbling experience to realize that I thought I knew everything before entering the program. Through this experience, I realized how my way of dealing with conflict wasn't working and I needed to shift gears.

4. Business simulation with teammate in grad school.

The fourth turning point in my conflict pattern was through a business simulation with one of my teammates—also during my program—which became very intense. This particular teammate was very animated and had a fly-off-the-handle type of personality. I wasn't aware of it at the time, but afterwards I realized, in some ways, she behaved similarly to my mom when I was a kid.

During the business simulation, the conversation within our group started to get heated as we were trying to resolve the challenge we were presented with. This particular teammate became visibly upset in her voice tone and facial expressions. I made a humorous comment with the intent to ease the tension so we could get through the simulation. She took what I said very personally and became even angrier. Things got more tense and it was very uncomfortable.

Afterwards, as a cohort, we discussed what happened during this interchange between us. She acknowledged that in her real-life leadership role, she's not taken seriously by many of the male counterparts in her organization. She admitted taking what I said and thinking I was like the men she works with, who all believe they are better than she is.

What I learned about myself through this experience was that when things get tense, sometimes I use humor to deflect, instead of directly addressing the issue at hand. Without intending to, my humor may offend others like it did my teammate and prevent candid conversations from occurring.

The personality profile feedback and this business simulation in grad school both deepened my self-awareness and personal development while showing me that personal development is a life-long journey that often progresses in unexpected ways . . . if we're open to learning from it.

5. Forgiveness of those who've abandoned and bullied me.

One day, at a family gathering, my dad ran into the family member who had embezzled from him. The family member finally apologized to my dad, and my dad, being the kind of man he is, accepted the apology.

Afterwards, my dad told me what happened and asked me to also forgive him. He said, "Will, I feel good about the conversation I had with him and I want you to make your peace with him too." You see, the embezzlement not only affected my dad, it also greatly impacted me. As a kid, I had idolized this family member and trusted him implicitly.

I eventually did call the family member. I said, "I want to tell you that I forgive you." Initially he didn't know what I was referring to and he said, "What are you forgiving me for?" I said, "Well you screwed over my dad for one, and second, you let me down. When I was a kid, you promised to be my best friend forever [goes back to the whole broken promise thing with my mom]. I looked up to you and the choices you made told me you weren't who I thought you were: someone I greatly admired."

The first thing the family member said to me was, "Thank you. I've lived with regret and guilt on how I handled things." He was very grateful for my reaching out to him, and for my forgiveness. We didn't talk at length, but it was an important step forward for me to release the bitterness.

Years later, I saw him at a family wedding. He came over and sat down next to me. He took my hand and just held it. We sat in silence for a good bit, eventually I looked over at him and he was crying. I said, "Do you remember that time when I was a kid and you put me in a snowmobile suit so I'd be cushioned and you let me ride down the rocks into the rock pile?" He said, "Yeah." We both started laughing, and I said, "I want to get back to that relationship we had where I trusted you. I trusted that I wasn't going to get hurt because I had that snowsuit on. You always protected me."

Forgiving the School Bully

There are other people I've taken the initiative to forgive. Like the guy who bullied me in school. I approached him at a class reunion and said, "Remember me?" First thing he said was, "Can we go outside and talk?" I thought, "Oh great, here we go again. Don't punch me, I just had heart surgery!"

We went outside and he said, "I want you to know how sorry I am for how I treated you. I've carried this guilt with me for 40 years, but it wasn't something I could do over the phone. I had to do it in person. I just prayed to God for an opportunity to be able to tell you."

I told him, "That experience in high school helped me become who I am today. For one thing, I don't take crap from anyone anymore!"

The rest of the reunion weekend you would have thought he was my best friend and we had just been reunited after being separated. He was glued to my side and stuck with me the entire time!

6. A Wake-Up Call

Another pivotal turning point was in the last year. I had a near heart attack that led to heart surgery. It was a wake-up call that life is way too short to be testy and cranky. Being that way doesn't benefit anyone; it doesn't add years to our lives, it doesn't add days, it doesn't add minutes. Unresolved conflict only keeps us in this rut of mud and gunk that most of us so desperately want to get rid of.

Unresolved conflict only keeps us in this rut of mud and gunk that most of us so desperately want to get rid of.

What I Learned

My relationship with my daughter taught me to be self-aware of how I was making things worse in conflicts by blaming others and not listening to them.

But perhaps the most important thing I learned about myself from all of these events was to forgive. To be the first to take the initiative when there's been a wrong done to me, and to move towards reconciliation.

It was the relationship with my father and my own personal faith that gave me the courage to let go of the wrongdoing done to me. In some situations I was able to talk through what happened with some family members, and in other situations there was an unspoken acknowledgement ("I know that you know what happened and you know that I know") where we didn't rehash the events, we simply moved on.

At the end of the day, what matters most to me when it comes to conflict, is forgiveness, reconciliation, and restoration. My whole philosophy is that I'm going to share heaven with them someday, so I might as well get along with them on earth!

One of my friends had a conflictual relationship with his father growing up, and never forgave his dad before his dad died. My friend wrote a 20-page letter after his father's death and went to his father's grave. He lit the letter on fire and burned it. As he looked at the smoke from the burning letter, it symbolized my friend writing a letter to heaven to let his father know that he forgave his father and himself.

That's why I reach out to people in order to work through conflict, because I don't want to go to my grave being angry and bitter by not forgiving.

Productive Conflict Management Strategies

1. Forgiveness Is a Solution for Conflict.

When people wrong you, instead of holding onto bitterness, look to them as an example of who you don't want to be. Choose to reflect on the only thing you can control, your behavior.

2. Find Positive Role Models.

My dad helped me to make sense of events in my upbringing and gave me perspective. He's been my mentor not only in my business but also in choosing forgiveness, when it would be easy to hold onto resentment.

3. Ask Lots of Questions and then Listen.

Questions help you get to the root issue and bring to light an answer much more than telling people what to do. My daughter taught me the importance of genuinely listening so she feels heard and understood. The family member who embezzled from my dad asked questions to understand

> *When we finally put everything out on the table . . . that's when I felt like he really "got it," he understood what his actions did to me.*

the impact of his choices on me. When we finally put everything out on the table about how his choices impacted me, that's when I felt like he really "got it," he understood what his actions did to me.

4. Find a Faith That Grounds You to Do What Your Human Nature Doesn't Want to Do.

I couldn't have forgiven my mother, family members, or have the business I have today if it weren't for my faith. Forgiveness is nothing more than acknowledging that the past is never going to be any different. Faith helps me to implement forgiveness and grounds me to do what, in my human nature, I don't want to do.

The Family Factor:
Forgiveness as a Conflict Strategy

When you forgive, you in no way change the past—but you sure do change the future.

—Bernard Meltzer

When one's parents exhibit vastly different personalities and conflict management styles, the Family Factor can be complex. Will's father modeled an almost super-human ability to forgive. Whereas Will's mother's unpredictable behavior left him with a deep mistrust of others. Eventually, however, the dominant element of Will's Family Factor would come from his father, for Will's story underscores the power of forgiveness as a conflict management strategy. Despite having multiple people in his life who let him down and betrayed his trust, he ultimately decided he wasn't going to be defined by his past. He wasn't going to let past disappointments and holding onto the wrongdoing of others affect his future. We learn from his example two key lessons about forgiveness.

1. Forgiveness is a choice you make for you . . . *even if you never get an apology.*

Whether in your personal life or workplace, choosing to forgive creates a pathway to inner peace and freedom that counteracts the poison of resentment and bitterness. As in the famous saying, "Resentment is like drinking poison and expecting the other person to die," when you choose *not* to forgive it only harms you in the long run.

The reason is that you are not resolving anything. All you are doing is keeping the negativity alive. And that negativity burning inside you impacts how you behave toward others—including others who have never done anything to you.

The fact is you can't change the past. You can only change the present and the future. And the way to do that is through forgiveness. As Will says, "Forgiveness is nothing more than acknowledging that the past is never going to be any different."

Forgiveness is difficult. Human nature says to

- *not* forgive until the other person admits their wrongdoing;

- harbor resentment until the other person apologizes for what they've done; and

- make the other person "pay" for what they've done with money, incarceration, death, or all of the above.

Sometimes we need help to overcome our human nature. For Will, it was his faith that enabled him to forgive. For you it may be a mentor, a coach, a family member, a minister, or another spiritual advisor who inspires you to forgive. You may read a book, a story, or an article that depicts the power of forgiveness.

Forgiveness is a choice you make for you . . . *even if you never get an apology.* Find the support you need to forgive others even if, in your human nature, you don't want to. The benefits can be life-changing—from getting better sleep at night, boosting your immune system, and reducing your risk of heart attack to bringing you more calm and peace of mind. Forgiving others lowers stress hormones and can literally save your life!

2. Remove Your Blind Spots

One of the most powerful ways you can begin to forgive is by recognizing your own faults. No one is perfect, and that includes you. Once you recognize that you too have hurt others, that you have done things that others have forgiven you for, then you will find it easier to forgive others.

We all have blind spots—those habits and behaviors that are obvious to others, and unknowingly contribute to conflict and fractured relationships. Self-awareness is where we can start to remove blind spots and take responsibility for our own shortcomings. Through pivotal turning points in his life, beginning when he was a sophomore in high school, Will's story demonstrates the progression of his self-awareness over time to remove his blind spots. He showed a willingness to be honest and humble in recognizing how, unconsciously, he was guilty of exacerbating conflicts—for example, with his daughter and his grad school classmates. His willingness to recognize his own faults in relationships helped him to forgive others who hurt him.

Even if you apologize for your part in a conflict, others may be skeptical of restoring trust until they see you are making a concerted effort to change your behavior. They want to know that you "get it"—that you understand how your behavior or decisions impacted them and that you are working towards making sure it doesn't happen again.

Where do you, as a leader, even begin to rebuild employee trust and team cohesiveness when many employees are hurt, skeptical, and cynical that change is even possible?

It starts with your willingness to look within with honesty, humility, and vulnerability in order to remove blind spots and gain insight as to how your behavior is impacting your employees and co-workers.

Forgiveness Requires Discernment and Boundaries

Taking responsibility for your part of conflict is important in finding resolution and forgiveness. But what if you didn't do anything wrong? What if you were the victim of a malicious act or sexual misconduct at work? Choosing to forgive in these situations requires much consideration and is a highly personal decision.

A common misconception about forgiveness is that it implies offenders are willing to take ownership of their behavior and have ongoing accountability to prevent reverting back to previous behaviors. Ideally, the people who did the wrongdoing exhibit genuine remorse and take responsibility to permanently change their behavior. However, that's not always the case. Whether people take ownership of their behavior or eventually revert back to old behaviors, the key element of forgiving others is giving up the power these people have over you.

The following are areas to consider when choosing to forgive:

1. Acknowledge and Honor Your Feelings When You've Been Wronged

Forgiveness is a process, not a one-time event. Give yourself time to acknowledge how the event has impacted you and sort through the myriad of feelings you'll likely be going through. Oftentimes, there are layers of forgiveness that occur over time. By consistently honoring your feelings in this way—talking through them with a trusted advisor—you can eventually get to the point where you'll remember the event and won't be as emotionally charged by it.

2. Determine What Boundaries to Put in Place

Determine boundaries that protect you from further harm, and the degree to which you'll interact with the people you are forgiving. If they don't respect your boundaries, it's clear they're not taking ownership of their behavior and are likely to go back to old behaviors. Stand firm within your boundaries to protect yourself. It is possible to forgive someone and still interact with that person through the boundaries you establish. Everybody's boundaries aren't the same and depend on the person and situation.

3. Watch for Consistent Markers of Changed Behavior

When people are truly remorseful about poor choices they've made and how their choices have impacted others, they make a concerted effort to change. Lasting, genuine change takes time. Watch for consistent markers of changed behavior, when people do what they say they're going to do, before you trust again.

4. Determine What Will Be Different Before You Trust Again

Most people will become remorseful when they recognize they've hurt people or made a poor decision that negatively impacted others. Those who don't show remorse may have a character issue preventing them from taking responsibility for what they've done. Before you fully trust again, determine in advance what will be different about your relationship with the people you are forgiving going forward. Specifically identify which behaviors will be tolerated and which will not be tolerated. Determine what's best for you, even if others don't like your boundaries.

5. Be Aware of Signs of Manipulation Making "Their" Problem, Your Problem

People who don't take responsibility for their behavior or how their behavior impacts others tend to twist circumstances so they can put the blame on other people and not take ownership themselves. Simply put, they deny the reality of what they've done. Again, establish boundaries to determine the degree of contact you'll have with them, if any. Be clear about what you will and won't do, and know it's their attempt to manipulate and control you so they don't have to be responsible for their choices.

Forgiveness Can Lead to a Better Future

Will shows us that forgiveness can happen with one person, yet in order for reconciliation to occur it takes those involved making a concerted effort to restore the relationship.

In my coaching and consulting practice, I've had the privilege of witnessing restored relationships because both leaders and employees were willing to do the hard work involved in forgiving and reconciling strained relationships. In one case, it took humility and intentionality for all involved to work through difficult, uncomfortable conversations that ultimately led to restored trust in one another. This led to the rebuilding of a cohesive team, which didn't happen overnight. It took time to see if people would follow through with changed behavior. Gradually, employees' loyalty to the organization increased because leaders modeled owning their part of the conflict, and addressing the problem directly instead of ignoring it.

The same can be true of your team, if you're willing to do your part. Over time, trust can be built, forgiveness granted, and your team can get stronger. More importantly, you will have brought humanity into the workplace.

References

Drinking poison quote:
https://quoteinvestigator.com/2017/08/19/resentment/.
Accessed December 21, 2019.

"How to Know if Someone will Change." Emailed video from Henry Cloud, received January 11, 2019. Henry Cloud's website is https://www.boundaries.me/.

"Why forgiveness does not mean you have to trust." Emailed video from Henry Cloud, received July 27, 2019. Henry Cloud's website is https://www.boundaries.me/

Self-Reflection Questions

1. Who is someone at work—or more than one person at your work— that you're having a hard time forgiving?

2. What would you like those who have wronged you to understand about how their behavior has impacted you?

3. How would your interactions with these people be different if they took responsibility for how their behavior impacts you?

4. What might happen in your situation if you chose to forgive them as Will described . . . even if they never admit wrongdoing?

5. Describe a time when someone forgave you and the impact of that person's forgiveness on you.

Increasingly, command and control is being replaced by or intermixed with all kinds of relationships: alliances, joint ventures, minority participations, partnerships, know-how, and marketing agreements— all relationships in which no one controls and no one commands. These relationships have to be based on a common understanding of objectives, policies, and strategies; on teamwork; and on persuasion.

—Peter F. Drucker, Austrian-American
Management Consultant

CHAPTER EIGHT

Jeremiah Johnson's Story
Leadership Balance: Different Styles
For Different Situations

Chapter Summary: Jeremiah's story reveals how controlling behaviors impact relationships in both families and work lives. He gives us an inside look at how, in the quest to always be in control, we can end up giving away our power to controlling people. The secret is to take control when required; to recognize the limits of our control and the power of enabling others to take responsibility; and, finally, to avoid destructive power struggles at all times. In the workplace, just like in families, you can't change controlling people, you can only change how you respond to them. Jeremiah shows us how he made the choice to change his response.

The Best Day of My Life Was the Day My Parents Divorced

Growing up, our house was filled with arguing and tension from the constant fighting of my parents. Mom's way of dealing with conflict was "command-and-control" while Dad was more calm and even-keeled. He had a much softer approach and didn't like conflict. Mom was extremely intelligent, but very controlling. One way to summarize the difference between how my parents dealt with conflict was that Mom would *tell* you how something makes you feel, Dad would *ask* you how it makes you feel. Dad would want to talk things out and come to a consensus, whereas Mom would tell you what to do, even how to feel. The best day of my life was the day my parents divorced; I was 19 at the time.

Both of my parents worked full-time. As the oldest of several kids, I was often put in charge at a young age to look after my younger siblings. It wasn't uncommon for me to organize dinners and attend teacher conferences for my siblings when my parents were working. I learned to handle conflict as I was trying to manage my brothers and sisters, primarily by taking charge, bringing order to the chaos, and getting things done. It was ingrained in me that as the oldest, I had to take control and couldn't run away from anything. After high school, I'd had enough. I bypassed the opportunity to go directly to college; instead, I got out of the house, went to work in a large factory, and attended college off-shifts. I wanted to escape.

How My Family Shows Up in My Office

When I first started out in management, I thought, in order to be a strong leader, I was supposed to be like my mom, "command-and-control." Over time, I learned two things that made me realize how control could be an illusion.

First, as I was promoted and was given added responsibilities, I realized I couldn't know everything. No matter what my authority position was, I couldn't do everything myself. My success depended on the success of my employees, and the "command-and-control" leadership style didn't work well in gaining the cooperation from my employees. That's one of the first times I realized that if I was going to be effective as a leader, I needed to change my approach.

My second realization was that I responded to controlling behavior from others by trying to regain control by taking on additional responsibility. The result was the opposite of what I intended. By letting controlling people draw me into a power struggle, and responding to them by trying to take responsibility, I was *actually giving* them control. The result? I was letting them take control of me! That was eye-opening for me.

Pivotal Moment

A pivotal moment stands out for me when I became my own person and shifted my leadership style from exclusively command-and-control to being a consensus builder—and avoiding the trap of responding to controlling people.

In my late 20s, my wife and mother got into an argument at my mother's house around Christmas time. I don't remember the issue. I'm sure it was something trivial that my mom wanted to have her way about. During the disagreement, I stood up for my wife. My mom, in turn, told us to leave. We didn't speak to her for about a year. When the holidays rolled around again, we were invited to Mom's house for a Christmas gathering as if nothing had ever happened.

The incident was never talked about again. While I would have liked to address the incident from the prior year with my mom and clear the air, I also knew from her past behavior that she couldn't handle it, and it would end up in another argument. That whole event gave me perspective about choosing to be my own person and taking my own stand, or continuing to give her the power to manipulate how I felt.

Fast forward a few years later, I was at work and my boss was ranting and raving about some production that hadn't happened like he thought it should. I felt myself getting stressed and immediately feeling responsible for the problem, like I felt responsible for everything growing up. I wanted to defend myself and talk about what we could do to resolve the issue. Then literally, as if a light went on, I realized it was like talking to my mother. That's how she would behave. When she was in a situation she couldn't control, she would lash out with her anger. In a split second I thought, "You know, he's not my mother. He doesn't have to have the cords to pull emotionally with me." In that moment, I decided the only power he had was the power I gave him, not the power he had because of his position. I showed respect for him, while at the same time released myself from being responsible for causing the production problem.

From that point on, I've been intentional about staying rooted in the issue at hand, asking questions and then dealing with the problem, rather than engaging in the perceived power struggle I was carrying around from my past family experiences.

It's not like I've got it all figured out, because I don't. I still get in situations where something will happen and I'll find myself giving others power because I'm taking their response personally. I've learned to catch this when it happens, by being in touch with my body, taking deep breaths, saying I just need a break, and taking a walk, which gives me clarity about the situation. I've learned it's about being in control of myself and coming back to the conflict, not about running away from it.

The Role of My Father

I attribute much of who I am today as a leader to my dad. While I've done the work, he has been my sounding board to make sense of events from my upbringing, and to shift my behavior from command-and-control to being a consensus-builder and building collaborative teams. My dad taught me that strength of character comes from being patient, understanding, and non-judgmental, and in listening rather than winning emotional competitions by dominating, getting angry, and taking control.

The most important thing my dad gave me was his sincere interest in me and the validation of my feelings. As an adult, we've had conversations that were instrumental in my rethinking my perception when I was growing up of my dad being weak. Unlike my mom, who just took control and told people what to do, Dad asked questions and tried to keep heated conversations from escalating. He taught me how to be comfortable with conflict and actually harness the energy of conflict for better understanding and better relationships. The skills he modeled, of asking good questions and truly listening to the answers, is how you get the true issues out on the table. He taught me that conflict can be a learning opportunity in developing team consensus to solve problems. When I began to look at conflict in this way, it was like a monkey off my back and I no longer avoided it, I embraced it.

From talking with my dad, I know we all have our experiences from growing up inside of us. When we're in stressful situations, we'll have a tendency to lean back on how we've been trained to behave as a little kid. I would act more like my mom because I grew up thinking I was supposed to be responsible, and command-and-control was the way to make things happen.

Over the years and again through conversations with my dad, I've realized that who I really am is more like my dad. I prefer engaging in conversations, asking questions, and listening. I've learned to lean more on who I am instead of fighting it. I felt like there was some rule or moral that was hammered in my head growing up, on how to be responsible. I've learned I can be responsible, without taking on the responsibility for others, and do it through consensus-building instead of command-and-control.

Leadership Balance: Different Styles for Different Situations

Looking back on my upbringing, I've come to appreciate that my parents did the best they could with what they knew at the time. It's been a process of both my own internal reflection, and numerous conversations with my dad, to come to this place of appreciating the strengths *both* of my parents gave me. When I was in my 20s, I didn't see it that way. I resented being put in a position of parental-like responsibility for my siblings and not being able to do usual teenager

Instead of only focusing on the negative aspect of my parents' behavior, I began focusing on what they taught me.

partying with my friends. By addressing that resentment with my dad, I see how my parents just didn't know how to work through their differences, and I learned leadership skills through the role I had in my family.

For example, I can now see how my mom came to be so controlling because that's what her dad was like. Having the perspective of looking at the family patterns gave me understanding, even compassion, for my parents. Instead of only focusing on the negative aspect of my parents' behavior, I began focusing on what they taught me. From my mother, I learned a great deal about handling situations very analytically and typically, non-emotionally. As a leader, sometimes you have to approach decisions that way, especially in emergency situations. From my dad, I learned how to ask good questions and really listen, in order to build consensus.

It was really exposure to both of those extremes as I was growing up that taught me how to be discerning as a leader, and when to use which approach. Now with over 40-plus years of leadership experience and encountering different circumstances, I have a better sense of when to use which approach. When there's an emergency, you've got to be command-and-control. When I want to get buy-in on a project and build teamwork, then I focus on asking questions and listening.

This doesn't mean that I avoid conflict. In fact, building a consensus often involves conflict, but as my dad taught me, the energy of conflict can be harnessed and used to arrive at a consensus.

And, under no circumstances, do I let controlling people dictate how I respond to a situation.

Productive Conflict Management Strategies

1. Retain Control: Own Your Response to Controlling People.

Depending on how you react to a controlling person, you may be giving them control that they don't really have. If you feel that you have to take full responsibility for something, or if you feel that you have to be defensive, you are giving up control. Remember that no matter how intimidating a controlling person may seem, they don't have any power that you are not willing to give them.

2. Release Control: Allow People to Be Responsible for Themselves.

If you grew up in a family where you were taught to be responsible for other people's well-being, it may seem that the only way to function successfully is to take control. I learned I could be successful and an effective leader by yielding control and empowering others to be responsible for themselves.

If, because of your family background, you feel the need to take control of every situation, it may be that the source of this need is internal, not external. In other words, you may fool yourself by saying, "If the situation is going to be resolved, it requires me to take control." In fact, it's not the situation that's pushing you to take control; it's the fact that your response to every situation is to take control. Be aware of blaming the situation for your bias. My need to take charge didn't necessarily reflect the requirements of the situation, but rather was my default behavior resulting from my background.

In a family setting, parents will keep tight and, as much as possible, total control over their children (hopefully adjusting this control to reflect the child's age and maturity). In a workplace setting, total control is an illusion; it's impossible to achieve. Even an overbearing, command-and-control boss has less control than he or she might believe. In my case, I had total control over my brothers and sisters. However, I eventually realized that I couldn't replicate this total control as a leader in my job, and that attempting to achieve this control was making work more stressful.

3. Discern When to Step in and When to Step Back.

One of the key attributes of an effective leader is the ability to discern between those situations that need the leader to step in and take control, and those situations that are better served by the leader stepping back and letting others take the initiative. It will turn out that most situations don't require leadership control when good questions are asked and people feel their ideas are heard.

4. Be Realistic About the Degree of Control You Have as a Leader.

It may seem like an oxymoron, but the higher your position in a company, the more you are required to give up control of the details. A machinist on a factory floor has complete control over his or her area of responsibility. The plant manager, however, can't achieve his or her responsibilities without the help of the workers on the factory floor. And the VP of manufacturing has to rely on all the plant managers and workers doing their jobs. Of course, leaders must engage and inspire those who work under them.

5. Ask Questions and Listen to the Answers.

Command-and-control leaders believe asking questions and building consensus is an inefficient waste of time. In essence, they are replicating the old parental standby, "Because I said so!"

The most effective and best leaders recognize that this "Because I said so!" attitude is counterproductive, and an inefficient way to lead. You get more from people if they participate in decisions. I learned this when I moved to a position in which I had responsibilities over areas I didn't have expertise in. I found that by asking questions and listening, I accomplished much more.

6. Harness the Energy of Conflict.

In family situations, when healthy conflict is avoided, it leads to anger, recriminations, and a breakdown of communication. In the workplace, command-and-control leaders have the same attitude about conflict and will not engage in it. If conflict occurs, these leaders will attack it with a vengeance. My control-driven mother did the same thing. I learned through candid conversations with my father that conflict can be constructive if it's handled correctly: that is, by asking questions, getting the issues on the table, and communicating openly and with respect. With this approach, you end up harnessing the energy of conflict, turning this energy into positive progress rather than negative warfare.

The Family Factor:
Change Your Response to Controlling People

As with Will, Jeremiah's parents exhibited opposite approaches to conflict. For Jeremiah, the core of his Family Factor was control. His mom dealt with all conflict through aggressive command-and-control behavior. His father, on the other hand, preferred consensus-building over command-and-control. During his upbringing, Jeremiah was unhappy with his mother's controlling behavior—but, ironically, he also came to believe that leadership required such behavior. Eventually, he learned that taking control was not always the best answer—but neither was letting others take power away from you. In the end, Jeremiah learned that the key to successful leadership was adapting to different situations appropriately—taking control when required, while delegating when possible. Most important, however, is the refusal to give up your power to others through their controlling behavior.

Perhaps you relate to Jeremiah's story about dealing with a controlling co-worker or boss in your work setting.

The good news is by gaining self-awareness of how you tend to respond to this type of person, you can recognize you have choices in how you respond and take back your power.

Organizational psychologist Henry Cloud provides insights on when you're allowing another person to control you. One of those insights comes by listening to what you say in response to a controlling person. In your own words, according to Cloud, you'll hear clues in how (unconsciously) you give away your power.

For example, if you find yourself saying any of the following phrases, you're giving away your power:

- I had to . . .

- They made me . . .

- I didn't have a choice . . .

In contrast, if you can say any of the following phrases, you have kept your power:

- I wanted to . . .
- They encouraged me . . .
- The organization is open to my ideas . . .

The difference between a controlling boss and an empowering boss—literally, a boss that gives you the power, or lets you keep your power—is that the empowering boss recognizes that you have choices. The empowering boss encourages employees to think for themselves and bring out their best.

Granted, in some situations at work, if you want to stay employed or avoid a tarnished work reputation, you need to respect authority and comply with directives—in other words, you may have to accept being in a position where the first set of statements above applies.

Also, standing up to a controlling person is not always the best solution for you. You may have a boss who is so controlling that you know standing up to him or her will get you fired, so you decide that the payoffs of the relationship—whether staying employed, acquiring experience at a major firm, or any other payoff—are worth giving away your power. Note that *you* are making the choice: You are choosing the payoff over the power.

In Jeremiah's case, as he was growing up, he went along with his mother's command-and-control parental approach out of respect for her as his mother, and to avoid her having an emotional blow-up. Later, as an adult, when he found himself working for a controlling boss and had the "aha!" moment—"I realized it was like talking to my mother"—he had a key self-awareness revelation that enabled him to take back his power as a person; this was a turning point in his life and leadership.

> *I decided the only power he had was the power I gave him, not the power he had because of his position. I showed respect for him, while at the same time released myself from being responsible for causing the production problem.*

From that point on, I've been intentional about staying rooted in the issue at hand, asking questions and then dealing with the problem, rather than engaging in the perceived power struggle I was carrying around from my past family experiences.

This revelation enabled Jeremiah to see controlling behaviors for what they are: attempts to get people to do what the controller wants. Through this incident, as well as ongoing conversations with his father about his upbringing, Jeremiah developed the skills to recognize who owns a particular problem, and thus avoid getting caught in a power struggle.

By making the Family Factor connection that his mother's controlling behaviors were showing up in his boss's behaviors, Jeremiah transformed his leadership conflict style from controlling to empowering. This is what a leader's conflict pattern transformation can look like when leaders gain awareness of how their work life is an extension of their family upbringing. Leaders benefit, employees benefit, and the organization benefits.

Reference

"Say No to Manipulators Without Feeling Guilty." Emailed video from Henry Cloud, received August 30, 2019. Henry Cloud's website is https://www.boundaries.me/.

Self-Reflection Questions

1. In what ways might you exhibit controlling behaviors?

2. In what ways have you allowed yourself to be controlled by others?

3. If you're currently in a work situation with a "controlling" person, what actions could you apply from Jeremiah's story to your situation?

4. What might be the conscious or unconscious "pay-off" that you're getting from this "controlling person"? List as many as you can think of, i.e. acceptance, approval, paycheck.

5. What is one step you could take to own your power?

Note: If you're the recipient of extreme forms of controlling behavior such as bullying, abuse, or harassment in the workplace, take action to protect yourself, such as calling your employee assistance program and/or visiting your human resources department.

Nothing ever really goes away until it has taught us what we need to know.

—Pema Chodron

CHAPTER NINE

Grace's Story
Navigating Difficult Relationships Through Boundaries

Chapter Summary: Grace grew up with two extremes of how conflict was handled. One extreme was highly emotional and "in your face"; the other was the opposite extreme of avoidance. Her story describes how she stayed in an important (and difficult) personal relationship by implementing boundaries. The result was a healthier relationship within her family. She also applied those same skills to her leadership style, which contributed to a high-performing culture for her employees.

Two Cultures, Two Extremes

Conflict in my family was handled with extremes. My mother was Italian and grew up in an "in your face" Italian culture. My father was British and didn't deal with conflict at all. He was very reserved and constrained. When I was growing up, Dad was an alcoholic. He wasn't a mean drunk, just became quiet and sullen most of the time. My parents didn't fight often, but when they did, there was a meanness or spitefulness about it that brought a fair amount of passive-aggressive behavior between them, mostly from my mother. She was a classic "triangulator," meaning she would talk about my dad negatively to my brother and me. Rarely would she speak directly to my dad about whatever she was upset with him about. I didn't see my parents resolve conflict; it just kind of lingered as tension between them.

After I left home to go to college, my parents went through a major upheaval. My father went into recovery with his drinking and his sobriety changed the relationship between my parents. They made a lot of effort to restore their marriage through counseling and 12-step recovery work. Their relationship improved. My father worked at speaking up for himself—becoming very effective at dealing with conflict both at home and in his own workplace. My mother, on the other hand, still had a tendency to be emotionally impulsive, fly off the handle, and never really deal with conflict directly.

My Conflict Style

Growing up, my ability to cope with conflict wasn't particularly healthy. As a younger person I was highly rebellious. I did what I wanted to do, regardless of the consequences—especially those that might impact others. My conflict style was a combination of using humor to defuse tension, and shifting the focus. I probably didn't realize it at the time, but I was trying to control the situation by avoiding addressing the real issue. How I dealt with conflict really depended on the situation and the people involved.

The only emotionally safe person for me, especially as I became a teenager, was my paternal grandmother. We did not speak much about my dad's drinking and my mom's emotional outbursts, but she provided a protective cover for me when she was around.

A Turning Point

Two events created the turning point for me, for learning to handle conflict in healthier ways. The first was several years ago, when my mother came to live with my husband and me to recover after a surgery. The anticipation of this extended visit made me realize I needed to do something very different in my relationship with her. Despite the high level of dysfunction that was present with my mother, I decided to be more intentional in figuring out how to stay in a relationship with her without getting caught up in the dysfunction.

I learned how to set good boundaries and stick with them so that every interaction with her didn't end up in conflict. The landmark book *Boundaries* by Henry Cloud and John Townsend, and another book they coauthored called *Safe People,* offered very practical help in setting and holding healthy boundaries with people who may be unsafe. I used their ideas with my relationship with my mother, and now I apply them to all of my relationships.

The second event that impacted how I changed my conflict style was a quote by a pastor, John Wesley, from the 1700s. He stated, "Conflict rightly worked through can achieve a higher state of grace and trust." That quote resonated with me. Conflict isn't something to be avoided. It's something to be engaged. In a broken world, we'll inevitably have conflict and differences with people, especially those we're in close relationship with, both at home and at work.

I pondered the John Wesley quote for a long time and it shifted my own worldview around conflict. It took me a long time to digest and comprehend the meaning of that quote and apply it to my life . . . and I don't know that I always live it out perfectly. But, in terms of my understanding of it, I often see that it's true. I'm realistic that living out

> *With every interaction with my mother, I was intentional in being present with her without engaging in the old dance that was deeply ingrained in both of us.*

that quote requires the other person or people I'm in conflict with to be willing to work through the issues with me. If there's not some degree of relational connection, it's probably not going to be possible to achieve that.

With every interaction with my mother, I was intentional in being present with her without engaging in the old dance that was deeply ingrained in both of us. For me, it was not bolting out of the conversation when I saw a situation differently than she did. At times, I would literally say to her, "I'm not willing to engage around this," which wasn't often received well, but I did it anyway. Boundaries helped me to decide in advance how I was going to react to my mother's emotions, and to stop allowing her to dictate how I felt or responded to her.

How My Family Shows Up in My Office

There are certain interactions that are emotional hooks for me that probably stem from my upbringing—for example, when employees or co-workers come to me in a way that I call "locked and loaded." They're attached to their position and not open to hearing anything different. My tendency then is to be dismissive. In those instances, I'll do what's best for the organization and for the other people involved, regardless of how those employees or co-workers may feel.

In those instances, it's like the "locked-and-loaded" person reminds me of the way my mom dealt with conflict, putting my mom in my office. Maybe there's still a part of me that rebels by dismissing the person and doing what I think is best, just like as a teenager, I did what I wanted to do.

I'm beginning to get better at recognizing when that happens, and stepping away or setting boundaries with that person. It's not helpful to ramp up an emotionally charged situation. My responsibility is to check myself and how I'm reacting and responding to a particular situation, and to identify, "Okay, what's the hook here?"

Sometimes that requires me to push the pause button in the middle of an interaction and say, "Look I'm not prepared to deal with this right now. Give me a day or a few hours to step back and gain perspective." Then I'm able to make the needed shift to engage more fruitfully. Having the freedom to hit the pause button has been very important for me because I recognize not everything has to be worked out right in the moment.

I know that the way my family modeled conflict was less than ideal. We avoided talking to work through differences. I have learned how quickly unresolved conflict can devolve when it is not addressed and worked through. Those experiences have compelled me to intentionally learn healthy boundaries, and that has positively affected how I lead. I've come a long way in developing healthy conflict skills from being rebellious, avoidant, and controlling in my younger years!

When to Engage in Conflict and When to Let It Go

Figuring out when and how long to try to have a relationship with someone who is highly adversarial is really hard to do. I'm personally challenged around this because I'm an optimist, so I tend to want to hang on to relationships; I think everything can be fixed and the reality is, it can't. Part of my own growth and maturity, and effort to change my family patterns, has been recognizing when something's not working anymore and being willing to abandon it or let it go.

I read a lot of leadership development books that have been very helpful in understanding what keeps me hooked and hanging on too long in relationships. I made the conscious choice to stay in a relationship with my mother even when she continued to be highly emotional because I recognized that there were particular topics where it made sense to engage with her, even when I didn't agree with her perspective. Again, having good boundaries was key in how I navigated those topics. I also recognized that certain topics can't be resolved with a person who isn't emotionally healthy. That doesn't make them a bad person; they simply lack the skills. But you can create a different kind of condition, where something new emerges in the relationship. And that possibility makes it worth the pursuit, if it's someone you care about. And then, there are other people, you just say, "Done. No energy going here. Not interested."

One of the most impactful learning experiences I've had about when to engage in conflict and when to let go is that without a relationship and some kind of mutually shared connection, resolving conflict well is often extraordinarily difficult. There has to be some of kind of mutual caring about one another as people. We may disagree vehemently about an issue, but if we care about one another and care enough to want to work through the conflict, the likelihood of getting to the other side of it is higher. Sometimes it may mean bringing in a third party who can mediate for that conversation to happen, which can be very helpful because it may not be resolvable between just the two people.

Creating the Conditions for Healthy Conflict

In my role as CEO, I'm very intentional about creating a work culture where people feel safe to bring differences forward so healthy relationships can develop. Perhaps this inner drive goes back to my upbringing, which was often the opposite.

Creating the conditions for a deep appreciation and valuing of the other person, even when you don't agree, is very important to me. When differences arise, I don't hesitate to encourage my employees to bring them to the surface and work through them. I also have very little problem with people disagreeing with me. I think disagreement is healthy when you allow people to express a differing opinion, work through it, and come out on the other side of the disagreement even stronger in the relationship.

As a staff, we work through things real time and try to deal with differences as they emerge. We deal directly with each other and are intentional about not triangulating (talking about them to others). I saw triangulating happen in my family when my mother would talk to my brother and me about issues she had with our father. It was very awkward as a kid to be in that position, and wasn't fair to my father to not hear my mother's concerns directly from her.

If our team comes to a point where we're not able to move past the disagreement, I might bring in a trusted third person to add perspective and help us work through the conflict. Sometimes we can't see what we can't see. Growing up, I wouldn't have tried to work out differences with my mother because she was so emotional. Today, as a leader, I've learned the skills to navigate emotional conversations.

At our organization, we're also intentional about distinguishing between forgiving and restoring trust. For example, forgiving someone is a matter of the heart. Immediately trusting after an offense usually takes time, until you see evidence of changed behavior.

I recognize conflict can't always be resolved. If the person you are in conflict with is unwilling to do the work, or is lacking in empathy or awareness of how his or her behavior is impacting others, it may not be possible to resolve or work through the issue immediately. Ultimately healthy conflict enhances how people work together. When people are at odds with one another, it drains energy from the work environment, which impacts relationships and productivity.

What I insist on is, "Don't talk about the person, talk to the person." As a leader, if an employee comes to me and has a problem with a co-worker, it's as if they want to put the monkey on my back saying, "You're the leader, so you deal with this person." The reality is, I may not have an issue with that person. If there's an issue between two people, I encourage them to attempt first to work through it. If they need my help after they've tried, I'm happy to be a resource, but I'm not going to take responsibility for someone else's problem.

The only exception may be if the person doesn't feel safe speaking to the co-worker, such as in a bullying or harassment situation. Otherwise, as a leader, I believe we do employees a disservice if we don't encourage them to develop healthy conflict resolution skills.

Depending on the nature of the issue, usually something new emerges out of a difficult conversation that is better than one person getting their way; it's about improving on what we are trying to accomplish *together*, focused on our common goal. That's the healthiest outcome of conflict!

Boundaries make it clear to each of us which behaviors are acceptable and which behaviors cross the line.

Developing Conflict Skills

In my own observations of the most successful leaders, CEO's, and presidents, I know very few who work through conflict well. Whether for business or personal reasons, they lack the ability to address differences. It's usually not a priority until it's an immediate need and then it ends up requiring more intense intervention.

Instead, if they created the kind of culture consistently where trust is built, relationships matter, and conflict is welcome—not mean-spirited, spiteful conflict, but rather healthy conflict—and there are good systems in place to support people working through that conflict . . . *that* creates a great place to work!

I often see organizations that lean strongly on grace, where there's all kinds of forgiveness in the system, but that means people are getting away with bad behavior; or organizations blindly (and unwisely) trust everyone . . . and people are getting hit over the head all the time, so there's constant tension.

Leaders need to be willing to invest in developing conflict skills, and getting good at it themselves. Lord knows there's plenty of opportunity to practice!

Productive Conflict Management Strategies

1. If a Conflict Can't Be Worked Out Over Time Between Employees, as a Leader and CEO, My Primary Responsibility Is to the Health of the Organization, not to the Individual.

I need to intervene in the case of poor behavior to protect the well-being of the culture. The system is going to keep doing what it's doing, unless I step into it and disrupt it in some way to make a change or make something different occur.

2. Let Employees Go if They're Not Willing to Own How Their Behavior Impacts the Team.

I'll try to work with them, but I won't tolerate employees who refuse to take responsibility for their actions. It's the necessary role of the leader to bring an end to something that's causing damage to the culture, whether that person is aware of it or not. It's never easy and should be viewed as a last resort, but sometimes it is absolutely necessary.

3. Make Efforts to Use Clear Boundaries to Stay in Relationship with Difficult People . . . And Be Wise About When You Should Step Out of a Relationship that Has Become Toxic.

There are no quick fixes for developing healthy conflict skills. Behaviors, starting from the top, have to be embedded in the culture of the organization. Create the conditions for appropriate relational connections to be built so that when differences emerge, the right stuff is there to allow people to work through them.

4. When Conflict Occurs, Make a Commitment to Move Forward, Even If You Haven't Come to a Complete Resolution on the Specific Issue.

When we have shared understanding of points of view, even without agreement, almost inevitably something new emerges in the relationships. Even if people never agree, they find places of common ground when places of shared understanding are found.

5. Know "Which Hills You Are Willing to Die On."

Recognize when a conflict isn't worth pushing into, even if you don't get your way. And then be genuinely supportive, even though you see the issue differently. We're not going to resolve every conflict.

6. Be Open to Revisiting, in the Future, Decisions that Were Once Contentious.

Rarely are decisions "one and done." We think sometimes if we don't resolve it perfectly today, it'll be a mess forever. In reality, small shifts and small compromises can move something forward, recognizing that there are lots of dynamics that we can't see yet that come into play as a decision unfolds. Be willing to live with the decision for a while, see how it works, and revisit it if needed.

7. When Addressing Disruptive Employee Conduct, Describe the Impact They're Having on Co-Workers and the Culture.

Recognize their impact is probably not their intent. One good way to see if a person is ready to do the work to resolve differences is if they are willing to "own their impact." My mother would often say to me, "You are misunderstanding my intent." This puts the responsibility of the issue back onto the person who has been impacted, and fosters shame and confusion. If a person is able to say, "That is not what I intended, but clearly I have impacted you negatively, I want to understand," then you have a much greater chance for working through an issue.

The Family Factor:
Self-Reflection Enables Self-Correction

Grace's Family Factor was a combination of her mother's highly aggressive behavior and her father's avoidance of conflict through alcohol. Her response was to fight back: when faced with aggressive behavior from others, she was not going to retreat. Over time, she became aware that being battle-ready was not the best response for conflict situations, and developed an alternative path to resolving conflict that centered on instilling boundaries in relationships.

Grace's transparency of acknowledging her journey from being rebellious, avoidant, and controlling in her younger years, to developing healthy conflict management skills as a leader, reveals how with effort, productive conflict skills can be learned.

Grace's story shows us that changing conflict patterns from your upbringing starts with the willingness to be vulnerable with oneself through what Sam Horn, author of *Take the Bully by the Horns: Stop Unethical, Uncooperative, or Unpleasant People from Running and Ruining Your Life*, refers to as self-reflection and self-correction. In her book, Horn describes self-reflection as the ability to reflect on the situations that trigger you emotionally (including those that stem from your upbringing), and to apply this self-awareness to make self-corrections in how you manage conflict today.

In the work setting, when you have co-workers, employees, or a boss who you struggle to get along with, rather than avoid, yell, finger-point, or leave, ask yourself, "What else can I do? I have to work with this person, I can't control what they do or don't do. What I can do is set boundaries." Boundaries are a self-correction choice you make in order to maintain work relationships and still be productive. Like Grace, whether at home or at work, the key to self-reflection and self-correction is making a conscious effort to look at how you can respond differently to prevent conflict from escalating. It also includes asking yourself, "How might I unknowingly keep conflict going?" or "What part do I play here?"

By applying self-reflection and self-correction through boundaries to the workplace, you

- set clear expectations;

- allow others to make their own choices without fixing or rescuing;

- follow through with allowing natural consequences to occur from the choices others make, so that they experience the logical consequences of those choices;

- free yourself from trying to control others or letting others dictate how you feel; and

- take responsibility for the only person you can control: you.

So often relationships are cut off or people leave jobs they love before making the concerted effort to self-reflect, address the part they play in the conflict, and make self-corrections. Leaving is always a choice. As the Pema Chodron quote states at the beginning of this chapter, "Nothing ever really goes away until it has taught us what we need to know." If you don't learn how you contributed to the conflict or considered how you can grow from this experience, you're likely to repeat that same pattern in future relationships, including with a future employer.

I recognize there are times to end a relationship or leave a toxic work environment—such as when you've made a concerted effort to improve the relationship, and the other person doesn't respond to your boundaries and attempts at reconciliation. Also, when there's abuse and harassment. Even in these scenarios, no matter what conflict or difficulty you're facing, take the time to self-reflect so you gain the self-awareness to protect yourself and have healthy relationships going forward.

> *If you don't learn how you contributed to the conflict or considered how you can grow from this experience, you're likely to repeat that same pattern in future relationships, including with a future employer.*

Through her willingness to self-reflect and recognize her part of how she kept conflict going with her mother, Grace was able to self-correct her reactive conflict tendencies. Today she responds much differently to conflict than in her upbringing. Setting healthy boundaries in her relationship with her mother has positively impacted her leadership style and created a high-performing culture for her employees.

Reference

Horn, Sam. *Take the Bully by the Horns: Stop Unethical, Uncooperative, or Unpleasant People from Running and Ruining your Life.* New York: St. Martin's Press, 2002.

Self-Reflection Questions

1. How well do you implement (and stick with) boundaries during conflict?

2. Consider someone at work you have difficulty getting along with; how might this relationship improve if you implemented boundaries?

3. How receptive are you to "self-reflect" and "self-correct" in taking responsibility for the part you play that keeps conflict going?

4. If you already set boundaries with difficult people, how likely are you to follow through with consequences when boundaries aren't honored?

5. Describe a time when you did follow through with boundaries that worked well. What did you learn from that experience?

Some bad things are going to happen, but more great things are going to happen. If you tend to see more bad than good, then you have to build that positive muscle in your brain much like an athlete does certain muscles to execute a certain move.

—Scott Hamilton, Olympic Figure Skater and Cancer Survivor

CHAPTER TEN

Ryan's Story
Release Family Baggage . . . Walk A Mile In Their Shoes

Chapter Summary: With many moves, little money, and minimal affection during his upbringing, Ryan could have become a bitter, angry man. Today, as a successful entrepreneur, he has consciously chosen to view circumstances from his parents' point of view and understand rather than judge. His story reveals how he chose to release his family baggage and be a leader who brings out the good in others by walking in their shoes.

Mom, Dad, Sister, and Brother—and This Other Person

Both of my parents were only children with a White Anglo-Saxon Protestant (WASP) background, meaning both were reserved and had a natural tendency to not address problems openly. They met during WWII. My dad was in the Army Air Corps and was stationed in England when they met. After they married and moved back to the States, money was tight and we moved several times throughout my childhood.

My parents didn't show much affection toward each other or me. It's not like there was friction between them. I think it was more the way they were raised: a public display of affection just wasn't something that was shown by them or the way they talked to each other. Even though Mom had the British reserve and stiff upper lip, I felt more empathy from her. Dad was more distant, not cold, but just kind of nothing in terms of affection. I can only remember one time when I heard my parents fight and the issue was never talked about again, to my knowledge.

I would describe my mom, dad, brother, and sister as the family unit, and I was this other person sort of floating off in space on the side. I was an only child until I was seven years old, when my brother was born; two years later my sister was born. Prior to my brother being born, I had a sense of belonging to the family. I got lots of attention and remember doing things with my parents. One time my dad took me into the projection booth in one of the movie theaters that he managed. It was a big deal for me to be in the projection booth because I got to be with my dad! After my brother and sister came along, doing things with my parents was over.

Throughout my childhood, I knew I was loved, even though my parents never said or showed it. It's not like I was abused. I sincerely believe my parents weren't aware of how much more attention they gave my siblings than me. I understand now how overwhelmed they were with providing the basic necessities and working to make ends meet. From their perspective, they didn't have to worry about me because I became self-sufficient after my siblings were born. At the time I don't think I understood why I didn't get more attention from my parents. It was just the way it was. That's all I got.

Believe it or not, I don't hold any grudges against my parents or my siblings. I understand my parents grew up during the Depression and the beginning of World War II, so it was tough for them growing up too. My mom grew up in a country that was under constant bombardment for most of her teen years. Though I wish things would have been different for me growing up, it was just the way it was. All of us are a product of our environment and times . . . and I'm a product of mine.

Conflict Was Avoided

My parents didn't address conflict directly; it just wasn't something done during that time era. After my siblings were born, I became very independent because they were younger and had more needs than I did. From a young age, I remember keeping very much to myself.

For example, if I was upset about something, I would take it out on inanimate objects, like punching something. I never talked about what was upsetting me. At other times I would use humor to ease the hurt, and then life went on. I remember a few times my feelings were hurt when my brother or sister would break something of mine. My parents didn't discipline my siblings for what they had done, and the feeling from them was, "Oh well, that's the way things are." One of my belongings they broke was a model I had spent a lot of time putting together. My parents never said anything about it or acknowledged my hurt; it was just "too bad." It was extremely disappointing. Looking back now, the lack of acknowledgment from my parents about the impact of my siblings' behavior on me probably reinforced why I didn't talk about my feelings.

My parents let me come and go as I pleased as a teenager; I wasn't supervised or even expected to be part of family meals. I often broke the driving curfew and it wasn't unusual for me to come home at two in the morning. My parents never said anything about coming home late. I had some traffic accidents, but even then, they weren't as concerned about me or whether I was okay. They seemed more concerned about getting the money to fix the car. That's an example of how I learned not to expect any emotional support from my parents, and at the same time I understood, from their vantage point, that money was really tight.

I didn't spend much time at home. I wasn't into drugs or breaking the law, just out with my friends hanging out. It seemed like there wasn't much to come home to. Even though I had a lot of friends, I had no best friend. I knew lots of kids, got along with them, but I was never a best friend to anyone.

My Relationship with My Parents as an Adult

When I was 35, my mom died unexpectedly. She was in her early 50s. It was tough because I was just starting to connect with her as an adult. At the time, I was living in another state over 2,500 miles from my parents, and had recently started a new job. I flew home to be with my dad to help him through the funeral.

Even though my dad and I never had heart-to-heart conversations, I always knew, deep down, he was a man of character. Being able to talk about feelings or give encouragement just wasn't who he was. We did get to the point where he could say, "I love you," and reciprocate a hug with me initiating it. To this day, Dad doesn't know much about me as a person, because we never had conversations beyond a surface level. It seemed like he gave the best parts of himself to people outside the family. He was always volunteering for all kinds of things, from the fire department to the church choir. He was one of those who got along great with all kinds of people. For whatever reason, he didn't have a way to bring that warmth back into the family.

How My Family Shows Up in My Office

In my first professional job, I was hired two weeks after a large group was hired. The larger group went through the formal training together. I came in by myself so they basically said, "Here's the book, go figure it out." I had no formal training for my job responsibilities so I had to teach myself. Then I kept getting bounced from one work group to another because of the way the work was laid out.

I had nine different supervisors in less than five years. When you keep changing bosses that rapidly, there's no connection with any of them. None of the supervisors tried to help me develop in my position(s). I saw all the people around me, who started at the same time as I did, getting promoted, and I wasn't. It was simply because there wasn't anybody to advocate for me . . . or to be my champion. I was unattached, just like I was in my family. It was a continuation of my life up to that point.

Over the years of my career, I've dealt with many examples of corporate politics—the internal power struggles that go on within a company. Most of the time, I tended to be on the side of the fence that wasn't winning the power struggle. I often got overlooked and stepped on so others could get ahead. In one particular job, I was fired because, in my role as an auditor, one report revealed major

> *The circumstances in my family upbringing taught me how to have an inner drive, to be resilient.*

problems that were disasters waiting to happen. But they were tied to the CEO-in-waiting, so the company buried them. I was the bearer of bad news and the scapegoat of the problem.

Just like in my family, when I was overlooked, I learned to pick myself up, dust myself off, and keep going. I've done that multiple times throughout my career. The circumstances in my family upbringing taught me how to have an inner drive, to be resilient.

But I always had a lingering negativity in my perspective despite my perseverance—and this negativity was a bigger problem than I ever realized.

A key turning point in overcoming the negative mindset was a comment made by one of the co-founders of a startup company I was with. He simply said, "Ryan, you're always so negative."

It was like somebody took a 2x4 and "Bam!", hit me upside the head with it. It went right into my soul when he said it. In that moment, I realized he was right. I could see how my negativity was working against me. Up to that point, I realized, I did have a tendency to be negative. I decided right then and there to change my outlook, and I did.

What Helped Me Change My Negative Mindset

Underneath, I've always believed in myself. If I decide I don't like something about myself and need to change it, I do. I've dedicated myself to constantly being able to evolve throughout my life. There's something inside that drives me when I'm aware of what I want to change, and I discipline myself to turn it around. Awareness is half the battle. Once I become aware, I do whatever it takes to change.

That particular comment from a co-worker about me being negative was the first catalyst to my slaying the dragon of pessimism, though it didn't happen until later in life. Since that time, for the most part, I've been a very positive person. The glass is at least half full, if not more, no matter what I'm going through.

The second catalyst in changing my negative mindset was a key phrase from the '60s that was very powerful for me, which was, "Walk a mile in my shoes." I've always taken that phrase to heart, both with my family and just about anybody else in the world. I try to take into account what's driving people:

- What got you to where you are right now?

- What did you go through?

- What have you dealt with in your life, in your family life, in your work life?

- What demons have you had to slay . . . because we've all got them.

That phrase, "Walk a mile in my shoes," has made me pause. It was eye-opening to have empathy for my own internal journey. What got me to where I am now is what I went through in my upbringing. I realized my negativity stemmed from feeling overlooked in my family. I often felt like I was just kind of put into existence and had little emotional connection to my family, or in work relationships. What's happened to me helped me to recognize that others have their own stories of what has happened to them that can trigger a rude or hurtful comment.

Now with everybody, I try to take into account that how we react to things such as conflict is from our experiences. I appreciate we all have to struggle with various ancillary things. Everybody goes through something, no matter how much money you have or don't have, or the color of your skin or your religion or whatever. We all have to deal with difficulties. Some people don't know how to work through them. They internalize the challenge and lash out at others.

Despite what happened in my upbringing, I chose to change the pattern of negativity to positivity. We all have that choice.

The Power of Forgiveness

For many years, I had heard from various sources about the power of forgiveness, but I didn't understand it. I decided to try it and see what happened. There wasn't one "aha!" moment or response to a particular event. Over time, I kept thinking about it and finally it clicked. And when I started to forgive, I felt free—I was no longer carrying baggage. Though I'm not happy with people for things they've done to me, I got to the point of saying, "I forgive you" . . . that was liberating. I could then put the wrongs done to me behind. Beyond being overlooked in my upbringing, I've had a lot of business misfortune throughout my life with colleagues, which hurt like hell, but I finally got to the point of forgiveness. Today, when I do forgive, I even have compassion for the other person and think, "I'm sorry you're the way you are and I'm going to move on, because I don't want to waste time in my life fretting about stuff that happened in the past when there's nothing I can do about it." I learn from it and move on.

Productive Conflict Management Strategies

1. Walk a Mile in Their Shoes.

Even if you believe you had a great upbringing, it doesn't mean your parents' behavior didn't impact you in some negative way. I grew up feeling like an outsider in my own family and my emotional needs were overlooked after my siblings were born. Regardless of what happened, I've made a conscious choice to view my circumstances from my parents' point of view and recognize that my parents had no malice towards me. I apply this same mindset and empathy to my leadership style by understanding others' point of view when differences occur that often stem from what's happened to them.

2. Develop Strengths from Struggles.

Since age seven, I was basically on my own emotionally. I chose to develop a resilient independence and self-sufficiency. This strength and self-reliance gave me a strong belief in myself to overcome a pessimistic outlook, and contributed to my success as an entrepreneur.

3. Forgiveness Is a Solution to Hurt and Resentment.

Forgiveness was liberating for me, and one of the solutions to my releasing resentment, hurt, and bitterness. Though I never felt like I had to forgive my family, I did work to understand them.

4. Work on Yourself Throughout Your Life.

Throughout my life, I have chosen to grow. It began with my resilience in my childhood and progressed organically in making a conscious effort to turn around my negative mindset.

5. People Are Not Stone (Change is Possible).

Children evolve and so can parents. I was able to develop a relationship with my mother as an adult, although unfortunately for only a short period of time because of her untimely death. On the other hand, my relationship with my dad didn't evolve as much. Through my initiating warm sentiments such as "I love you," my dad was able to say "I love you" in return, something my dad had never said throughout my upbringing. Though people may not change the way you would like, change is possible through your influence, though not guaranteed.

The Family Factor: Work through Conflict with Resilience

Ryan's Family Factor could have led to a lifetime of resentment and self-pity. Although never deliberately cruel, Ryan experienced a childhood with little affection from his parents, who showered their full affection on his siblings. Instead of resentment, however, Ryan emerged with an unbending capacity for resilience—a resilience that only strengthened over time as he learned through empathy how to forgive.

Diane Coutu describes three characteristics of resilience in a *Harvard Business Review* article, called "How Resilience Works," that demonstrates how Ryan brought resilience to his life without even realizing it.

> **1. Accept Reality**. *Resilient people see a situation for what it is in order to prepare and train themselves to act in ways to survive.*
>
> Ryan recognized the reality that his parents' behavior was a result of what they knew from their own upbringing and life events— the Depression, World War II, mother's home country under constant bombardment during her teen years—that had shaped their difficulty to show affection. While he wanted more attention from his parents after his siblings were born, he recognized his parents had limited time and energy due to their jobs and parenting responsibilities to his younger siblings. He learned at a young age how to accept reality and be self-sufficient.
>
> **2. Create Meaning**. *Look for opportunities to grow and have the perspective that challenges have purpose.*
>
> The phrase "Walk a mile in my shoes" gave Ryan the perspective to have empathy for other people. It allowed him to view difficulties in his life and difficult people by being curious about where they've come from and taking into account the story behind their behavior and choices.
>
> It also gave him empathy for himself as he realized that his tendency to have a negative mindset stemmed from feeling overlooked as a child. He viewed the challenges he went through since childhood as a catalyst to where he is today. He created meaning of his own struggles, by recognizing the importance of understanding that others have their own stories of what's happened to them—stories that can prompt a rude or hurtful comment.

3. Uncanny Ability to Improvise. *Think creatively about possible solutions to a challenge, even when you have few resources.*

After age seven, Ryan was often left on his own and he knew he only had himself to rely on. In order to overcome challenges, he learned how to improvise. Little did he know at the time that would become a fundamental skill he would use throughout his life:

- Throughout his career, Ryan has used the ability to improvise and find solutions to whatever challenges he faced.

- While growing up, he couldn't talk with his parents about his frustrations, so he improvised by seeking out alternative outlets to ease those frustrations (from humor to hitting inanimate objects).

- As a teenager, when he was allowed to do whatever he wanted with little to no supervision, he developed the ability to interact with a variety of people.

- Once in the working world, when he was left on his own without formal training in a new job, he taught himself what to do.

- When he received feedback about his negative attitude, he made a concerted effort to become positive.

Ryan built the positive (and resilient) muscles in his brain that Scott Hamilton references in the quote at the opening of this chapter to work through challenges and conflict in his life by projecting forgiveness and walking a mile in others' shoes. Imagine how much conflict in the workplace would be reduced if more emphasis was placed on taking into account what's behind a co-worker's or employee's behavior rather than judging them?

Perhaps there would be less judgment and more understanding of one another as people . . . and more conflict resolution instead of divisiveness.

Reference

Coutu, Diane. "How Resilience Works." *Harvard Business Review* 80, no. 5 (2002).

Self-Reflection Questions

1. What situation or person's behaviors at work are you currently having a difficult time "accepting the reality" of in the way Diane Coutu describes?

2. What meaning could you give to the above co-worker relationship that would allow you to see a greater purpose for, or a different perspective of this person's behavior?

3. How have you or someone in your family implemented the "uncanny ability to improvise" and think creatively about a challenge, even with few resources?

4. Describe a time that you overcame a negative mindset. How did you do it?

5. What might happen if you implemented at least one of Ryan's productive conflict strategies with the person you're currently in conflict with?

One can have no smaller or greater mastery than mastery of oneself.

—Leonardo da Vinci

CHAPTER ELEVEN

Jerry's Story
A Family Legacy Of Resilience Through Self-Worth

Chapter Summary: Jerry is an African-American businessman whose story is a testament to how a strong family foundation shapes a leader in ways that can't be learned in an MBA course. Through various events and setbacks that could have held him back from achieving his leadership potential, he persevered by taking responsibility for his behavior . . . including walking 45 minutes to work to get to his job on time. Jerry exemplifies how *not* to allow adversity or conflict to become what he calls a "standstill" in relationships, but rather to choose a resilient mindset by moving forward, tapping into your family legacy and self-worth, and not squandering opportunities to grow and learn.

I Got the Best Parts of Both of My Parents

As a single mother, my mom spoke directly. She didn't mince words! She taught my brother and me how to be responsible and resourceful. Her motto was, "Find a way to get what you want without stealing or getting into trouble *and take care of your business.*" She never had a GED or much of an education, but she was a hard worker. She worked nights and a part-time job during the day.

Even when she was tired, she found a way to be at my school sporting events, and was always available for us.

My parents split when I was around a year and a half. Even though we didn't live with my dad, he was always involved in my life. His fun-loving personality taught me life and people skills. He could talk to a cockroach, and could get anybody to open up to him so he could learn about their lives. When I was seven, he began teaching me how to cook. I remember him sliding a chair over to the stove for me to stand on, because I wasn't tall enough, so he could teach me how to cook potatoes. He said, "The pan is really hot, you've got to drop the potatoes in slow and steady." I'm like, "I've got this, I've got this!" I was so excited! When the first potatoes went in the pan there was a pop that I didn't expect and I dropped all the potatoes into the pan at once and got burned. My dad was nervous about sending me back to my mom's house with a burn! Mom understood and encouraged our time together. She knew the importance of my dad teaching me how to be a man, and never interfered with our relationship. I'm the best parts of both of my parents.

I appreciate that neither of my parents bashed one another. I often hear stories about kids getting caught between parents who don't get along, and how they hear negative things about one parent from the other. Gratefully, my parents never did that and remain good friends to this day. Even though I grew up in a single-family home, my parents never let what happened between them get in the way of how they treated us. It was always about the kids in the family and moving forward.

The Support and Influence of Extended Family

Besides my mother, I had strong black women in my life who raised me. My dad's aunt was very influential in my life. She was one of the first black professors at a university, and dealt with all the struggles and dramas that being a trailblazer brings. She always told me, "It doesn't matter what anyone else thinks." She taught me that if you know who you are, your values, your roots, you'll be okay. Don't let outside influences create doubt about who you are. Her resilience made an impression on me of how to persevere through tough times.

She was the consummate example of how to conduct and carry yourself, and taught those skills to my brother and me. For example, at a young age I remember her taking my brother and me to restaurants and encouraging us to order for ourselves and learn how to interact with people. My wife and I named our daughter after her because of her influence on both of our lives.

My maternal grandmother also had a big influence on my life. She had a persistent "you won't stop me" fighter attitude to overcome challenges. Her example is also ingrained in me to not give up, quit, or let others get the best of me. I largely attribute my success to the support that I've had from parents and extended family. Their words of wisdom helped me to get through tough times.

Taught to Represent My Family Well

I have a tattoo that says 20-20-20, which represents the 20 years apart between my uncle and father, and 20 years apart between my dad and me. It represents the monumental advantages that are given to minorities today, compared to years ago. I carry that message with me so that I don't forget the story of how my uncle couldn't get his dream job of selling shoes because of his ethnicity. It also helps me remember where I am today in my career as part owner of a restaurant. It makes me want to clearly represent where I came from and all the struggles that my family went through not so long ago. They never said to me, "Sit down, and let me teach you a lesson"; rather it was how they lived and the stories of how they overcame adversity that have shaped me. These stories helped me excel while in college and catapulted my success. They gave me a mindset of purpose, growth, and the desire to carry myself well, and to make sure I don't squander any opportunity. I also want to pass on to my kids the value of hard work to bridge the gap when life isn't easy because of ethnicity.

I'm the youngest member of my family by 13 years. It was advantageous that I could learn from my brother and uncles. I've made better choices in my life by learning from the mistakes I've witnessed from them.

Little Conflict in My Family Upbringing

I don't remember much conflict growing up. We didn't have any drama in our family, nothing that would make a good movie. If there was any conflict, I tended to respond to it with humor and became accommodating to ease the tension. I always found the bright side in the darkest spot. I learned how to be diplomatic and break down that exterior wall in people through laughter. If my parents did have disagreements, they dealt with it behind closed doors. When it comes to conflict today as an adult, I have no problem with it at all. I just don't bring it. I'm also not afraid to take a stand for what I believe in. I think the way I was raised taught me that no matter how people want to sway you, do what's right and be true to who you are.

While there wasn't much conflict in my family, I grew up with much diversity and adversity in high school. The school I attended was a melting pot of section eight housing and million-dollar homes. Some kids didn't know if they'd eat a meal when they got home, while some parents brought their kids pizza for lunch. I got to see the spectrum from the less fortunate to the highly fortunate kids. I wanted to be like the wealthy kids, to have the financial stability they had, and not have to worry about money.

Beyond the Family: SGORR

During elementary school in fourth and sixth grades, high school students from the Student Group on Race Relations (SGORR) came to speak to our classes. SGORR was (and is still today) a high school extracurricular program that promotes positive social relationships around issues of race and diversity. It made a positive impression on me, and starting in my sophomore year of high school, I was asked to be a facilitator for SGORR—which was a huge opportunity! As a sophomore, I was the youngest SGORR leader. SGORR gave me the skills to facilitate discussions with elementary kids on how to handle conflict and have conversations about diversity. I also learned how to coordinate meetings, stay organized, and go into the community to teach the SGORR principles and ideologies to adults. It was a great learning experience and prepared me for college and future leadership roles. SGORR especially helped me to spark difficult conversations, adhere to guidelines if conflicts arose, and mediate differences.

Moving into the Restaurant Business

In addition to SGORR, I always had a job as a teenager. I worked at an ice cream shop and by age 16, I became a shift manager. I learned how to count the money, order product, and close the building at a young age. It was a family-owned business and it was a big deal for a teenager to have the level of responsibility I had in running this little shop.

Down the street was an upscale Italian restaurant that made homemade products. The owner would frequently come to the ice cream shop and I always made his chocolate malt for him. He liked really thick malts and I was the only one who could make it the way he liked. One day I told him I wanted to go to culinary school and he invited me to come in for an interview. When I arrived, he led me into the basement of his restaurant and down through winding halls. I felt like I was in an Italian mafia movie! I finally got to his office, which had this big chair and all these screens showing the inside of the restaurant.

He didn't ask me to sit down. The first thing he said was, "So you want to work here?" I said, "Yes!" He said, "Why?" "Well I'm thinking about going to culinary school and I want to get some firsthand experience. I like what you guys do here, I think you'd be able to provide me with some of the experience I need." He said, "I like you. I'm going to give you a job." That was my interview!

I quit my job at the ice cream shop and worked every food station at the Italian restaurant to learn as much as I could. It was a big deal to have a high school student in the cooking stations. A lot of people at the restaurant questioned my ability, my skills, and judged me for being in that position. But I remembered what my aunt taught me: "Don't worry how people feel about you. Do what you can do in the position you're in." I'm forever grateful for the opportunity the owner gave me, and whenever I go back to my hometown, I thank him for giving me a chance that many kids I went to culinary school with didn't have. My classmates didn't know what it was really like to work in the kitchen, especially when you're working against the clock to get things done. In culinary school, you have all the time you want. I got the real-deal experience and it helped me tremendously in school.

Once I got to culinary school, I hit the ground running. My lab partner and I ran circles around everyone else! The teachers gave more opportunities to students who excelled. Because my lab partner and I showed initiative, adapted, and moved swiftly, we were given priority for bigger projects. Those were the qualities that helped me to graduate at the top of my class and both of us were students of the year!

How I Leveraged My Family Strengths: Overcoming Standstills

Conflicts often result in "standstills." Neither side wants to budge or give in. Getting to where I am today as a restaurant owner came with many obstacles and conflict "standstills" that could have held me back. The following lessons from my family and extended family helped me push through them successfully.

Standstill #1

My mom remarried when I was around ten years old. My relationship with my stepdad was respectful. Though he was a nice guy, I didn't really have much of a bond with him. After my brother went to college, it was hard for me. My brother and I had always had a good relationship. My brother's room was in the attic of the house and I decided to create a "hang out" space in his room with a TV. I didn't think it was a big deal, but my stepdad got upset with me for moving into my brother's room. He wanted me to move my things back to my room. We argued a little bit and he couldn't give me a reason why I couldn't stay in my brother's room. Now, keep in mind, I wasn't a kid that got into trouble; I was very responsible. My mom and brother were both okay with me moving into his room, but for some reason, he didn't want me to move up there. I shut down emotionally and was hurt that he wasn't allowing me to do something that was so simple. It was just space. Now I look back and it seems silly, but at the time, it was a big deal to me. I talked to my dad about it and he said, "Follow his rules, it's his and your mother's household." My dad is a very reasonable person and had an overwhelming amount of respect for my stepdad and vice versa. What my dad said made me realize, it wasn't my house. So I moved my things back to my room. From that point on, my stepdad and I just co-existed; we didn't talk for a while. My mom tried to get us to work it out, but we didn't get anywhere.

Shortly after this happened, my dad moved back to the area and eventually I moved in with him and my aunt. It started out just a few nights but since I hadn't seen my dad that much up to that point in my life, I wanted to see him as much as I could. There wasn't a big blowout with my stepdad, but now as I look back, I think there was something deeper going on. As a 17-year-old at the time, I didn't understand. I just wanted to be in my brother's room because we were close. Since my stepdad and I were at a standstill, I took my father's advice to respect my stepdad's authority and moved on.

Standstill #2

An incident happened when I was living at my culinary school apartment that became the second significant "standstill" that influenced how I deal with conflict.

My college housing was part of my tuition. I was wrongly accused, and about to face punishment for violating curfew while watching a playoff basketball game in my apartment. Like the first standstill, I didn't get what the big deal was since we didn't have school the next day. As my family taught me, I took a stand for what I thought was right. I was given the choice to take an online class for punishment or move out. I didn't make a scene and decided to move to an apartment I had to pay for. I had a roommate and a job. It would be a financial stretch, but it was doable for the remaining months I had left in college.

I felt good about standing up for what I believed in. I respected that we had differences and moved out, just like I had done when my stepdad and I had a standstill about my moving into my brother's room. I remembered what my dad said about the situation at the time with my stepdad: "It's not your place." I had to follow the rules just like I had to follow my mom and stepdad's rules in their house.

Shortly after this happened, the restaurant I was working at while attending culinary school closed. Then my roommate literally left in the middle of the night, leaving me with the full rent payment when I didn't have a job to cover it. It was early November, bitter cold outside, and I didn't have a car. A friend drove me in his car, without heat, from restaurant to restaurant putting in applications (this was before online applications). At the last restaurant, I said I was desperate and said, "I'll do whatever you need." On the spot, I was given an interview and got the job! That was how I got started with the restaurant I own today. They took me in like family and every time I see the general manager who hired me, I thank him for what he did for me. When you have those people in your life, you appreciate them!

As a new employee, I did what I was supposed to do and learned how to work all the food stations. Because I didn't have a car, I walked 45 minutes to work next to a very busy road where cars went 50 miles an hour, and there were no sidewalks. I'd jump across a fence to go over the road to shave 15 minutes off of my walk. I was always at work on time, with my uniform on, and gave my all. My goal was to get a car, but the wage I was making was just enough to pay my rent and give gas money to friends who occasionally gave me a ride to work.

Standstill #3

After several months of doing this, it began to weigh on me. By now I had graduated from culinary school. I asked my boss if he was pleased with my work and if there was anything I could do to improve. He said he was very happy with my performance and couldn't think of anything I could do to improve. I then asked him for a pay increase. He knew I didn't have a car, in fact some days he even passed me as I was walking to work and honked his horn but never offered me a ride. He said he couldn't give me a raise.

I was hurt and, again, just as my family had taught me, I respected his decision. I still maintained my same work ethic, walking to work, arriving on time, but finally decided to move on. One of my mentors who knew one of my goals was to become an executive chef suggested I transfer within the same restaurant chain to a location in my family's state, which is what I did. Within a week of getting my new job, my manager saw my skills and all that I could do. I got a raise that got me up to the minimum pay of what others at the restaurant were making. The raise validated that I made the right decision to move when I was at a standstill with my old boss.

Fast Progression Up

Since that time, I've become a classically trained executive chef and am known as the "go-to" guy to correct our restaurant culture. I've opened two locations, trained employees, and corrected longstanding problems. The Area Director was reluctant to hire me as a managing partner because of my age (under 30). However, because of how I've conducted myself and overcome challenges, I am now a part-owner of the restaurant.

How My Family Shows Up in My Office

Conflict in the restaurant business is around every corner and can erupt at any moment. When it happens, it makes me focus on what I learned in my family and what my tattoo symbolizes: to represent my family well, to have purpose and self-worth, and to not squander any opportunities. I've always tried to think about how my behavior would affect my environment. How can I help my employees overcome adversity and racial bias?

Many employees in the restaurant business come from rough upbringings, low socio-economic environments, little resources, or poor choices that landed them in jail. They didn't learn self-worth, or the importance of having goals. I don't say that to be disrespectful, it's just how it is. I understand the struggles they face from people I went to high school with and some within my own family; we didn't have a lot monetarily, but I was taught to represent the character I was given well.

My family upbringing is in my restaurant every day. The spectrum runs from employees who are struggling to get by to affluent customers who live a comfortable lifestyle. This reminds me of the kids I went to high school with, some from section eight housing while others lived in million-dollar homes.

I take the collective life skills I learned from my parents, extended family, and at SGORR to help my employees deal with adversity by encouraging them to tap into their self-worth and not squander opportunities. Even if some employees come from a tough upbringing and past, I encourage them to represent the strengths of who they are and the positive qualities they were given. I want my employees to be the best versions of themselves.

Just as my parents were available to me, I have an open-door policy with my employees. They are very open and honest with me and don't hold back. I want them to see me as a normal human being that they can relate to, and not just someone they have to report to. We are intentional about resolving a conflict quickly. I can't help how people feel, but I can help them resolve differences.

When it comes to my leadership team, I guess subconsciously, I've applied conflict management skills in the workplace from what I saw my parents model. Even if my parents disagreed about something, to my brother and me they were always united. Despite their divorce, they backed one another and I never heard them bash, blame, or undermine each another. I emphasize with my managers that we may not always agree, but we must work it out so our conflict doesn't affect our employees.

Productive Conflict Management Strategies

1. Create a United Leadership Team.

Even though you may have differences, or possibly not even like someone on your leadership team, learn how to get along with one another and be united in how you lead. We don't allow the cracks in our leadership team to affect our employees, just as my parents didn't allow their differences to affect my brother and me.

Even when conflict results in a standstill, I know I've done the right thing. I've followed rules, been honest, and I'm always on the side of what's right.

2. Conflict Presents Itself Every Day. Teach Your Employees How to Work Through It.

In my restaurant, my customers may be having a wonderful time with their family in the dining room, while back in the kitchen there's turmoil among employees. Most of us don't learn how to work through conflict in our family upbringing. I see that play out every day in my kitchen between employees who have arguments, and it affects how the kitchen runs.

As a leader, take the time to help your employees resolve disagreements by getting to the root of the problem. Being in the hospitality field, I strive to create a positive experience when people come to my restaurant. I want that same positive experience for my employees.

> *When there's conflict with employees, we go to a table in the restaurant, sit down, and figure out what's the root of the problem.*

When there's conflict with employees, we go to a table in the restaurant, sit down, and figure out what's the root of the problem. We literally get things out on the table and it cuts down on "he said/she said." By addressing the conflict, you'll not only have a better work culture, you're also investing in people to be a better version of themselves and develop stronger work relationships.

In addition, working through conflict keeps people in the right mindset. It can be difficult, and sometimes there are a lot of moving parts to make sure the conflict gets resolved. If it doesn't get resolved, it will eventually affect our customers or service delivery, and we don't want that.

3. Work Out Differences Over a Meal.

When I was growing up, I consistently experienced the value of being around a table. There's something positive that happens when people break bread together and share a meal.

Work out differences with your leadership team—that is, your managers or fellow leaders—away from the office and over a meal. Defenses go down and emotional outbursts are less likely in a public setting.

4. When Conflict Starts, Give Choices to Avoid a Power Struggle.

Mom kept life real. I remember as a kid going to the grocery story with her and being in the toy aisle. I told her I wanted a particular toy. She didn't tell me no; instead, she gave me a choice: "You can get this toy or we can have lights so you can watch TV." I put the toy back and never asked her again.

She was always realistic and put my wants into perspective. She avoided a power struggle with me by giving me a choice rather than "because I said so." I strive to be the same kind of parent and leader.

5. Have a Mentor.

From culinary school to now, I've always had a mentor who I could go to and run situations by. From these relationships, I've learned key leadership lessons that shaved years off my career progression. Sometimes as a leader, you don't know what you don't know or can't see what's obvious to others with more experience. Find a mentor you respect and trust, who will speak straight with you to help you see past your own blind spots.

6. Those Who Don't Have Goals Will Always Work for Someone Who Does.

The goal of getting a car is what pushed me to walk 45 minutes to work so I could earn it. The goal of becoming an executive chef is what propelled me to ask for a raise and move on when I didn't get it and knew I was worth it. One of my mentors once told me, "Other people will only take you as seriously as you take yourself."

I always encourage my employees to have goals and put in the effort to make their goals a reality. The effort to learn the fundamentals of showing up on time, caring about their appearance, and showing enthusiasm for what they do puts wind in my employees' sails to reach their goals. When I see my employees show effort, I reward them. I won't lose a hardworking line chef over a few dollars. I want my people to have goals and achieve them.

7. Know What Drives the Sustainability of Your Success.

My leadership skills primarily came from my family. My family upbringing gave me the character foundation to propel me forward in life. Being a good leader is about servant leadership—leading by serving employees in ways they want to mirror and emulate, like doing the right thing, taking responsibility, and modeling good character.

My personal family dynamic became stronger after I married my wife. She's the reason I am where I am today. I attribute her belief in me from the days when I was jumping over the fence walking to work to now. Her support and the way we work together as a unit with our two kids is the gift for which I am most grateful.

When struggles, conflict, and hard times come, and they still do, I appreciate knowing I have my wife beside me, my family behind me, and my kids around me. Together we figure it out.

8. Give to Your Employees What Can Never Be Taken Away.

I try to make my mark on my people by giving them the skills to move forward in life and overcome the challenges they've faced. I tell them if you decide to work here, you're going to become a better version of yourself. If you don't put in the effort, you won't last here.

To the extent that it's appropriate, I share how struggles and conflicts have shaped me and my leadership skills and how I got to where I am today. I want to inspire them. I haven't had it easy in my journey, but I've overcome monumental challenges *and they can too*!

One of the highlights of my job is watching chefs with a criminal background take their pure, raw talent and thrive. When they make that turnaround, they can see what a firecracker they were and where their life was headed. I encourage them to reach professional milestones, start a family of their own, be happy— the kind of things you can't put a price tag on. The real satisfaction I get out of my job is seeing my people grow. That's what's rewarding.

The Family Factor:
Take Responsibility for Your Response

Jerry's Family Factor, which draws heavily on the experiences and examples of both immediate and extended members of his family, is the recognition of the power of being in control and mastering your emotions. With each of the three "standstills" that he faced, he was in charge of what he said and did, which prevented conflict from occurring or escalating.

Unhealthy conflict can only occur when at least two people are caught up in reacting from their emotions of either fight or flight. When this happens, stress hormones flood the rational part of their brains, resulting in the tendency to say or do something they later regret. In this state, people tend to react with blame and defensiveness to justify their position, or avoid the conflict altogether and stop talking. This is what Jerry describes as a "standstill," when nothing can be resolved.

On the other hand, one person can choose not to take the bait to engage in a heated argument, but instead back away, accept the standstill, and stay engaged while remaining calm and composed. Conflict can be de-escalated once started, which is what Jerry did.

Whether at home or in the workplace, using self-control to consciously *choose* your response is an invaluable skill to have.

David G. Reynolds, in his book *Constructive Living*, states, "Feelings can be directly influenced by behavior." This means that if you don't feel like taking the high road but you do it anyway, your feelings will change and the situation will be defused or made calm.

Feelings can only run the show and emotionally hijack the situation if you let them. As soon as you react to what someone else does or doesn't do, says or doesn't say, you've given away your control. The difference between staying calm (responding) or reacting is a choice. Just like Jerry, you can control your response—your feelings—by the behaviors you choose.

The Drama Triangle

Here's a common scenario in the workplace and how to choose your behaviors wisely.

As referenced in Chapter 9, "triangulation" occurs when two people are in conflict and another person is brought in as an attempt to decrease the tension. Triangulation is also known as the "Drama Triangle," a model of conflict first identified by Dr. Stephen Karpman back in 1967. Within the Drama Triangle, Dr. Karpman identified three interchangeable roles people often take on unconsciously during conflict that creates tension, confusion, and drama. As you can imagine, Drama Triangles occur in both our personal and professional lives.

The three archetypal roles within the Drama Triangle are *victim*, *persecutor*, and *rescuer*. The victim is the person who feels he or she is being treated unfairly or wrongly by the persecutor. The victim's stance is often, "Poor me, look at what this person is doing to me!" For example, in a work setting, the persecutor can be a boss who's focused on results and getting projects done. To the victim, the persecutor's tone comes across as harsh and demanding. The victim perceives the persecutor as being condescending, when from the boss/persecutor's perspective, the employee/victim hasn't followed through on commitments to complete the project.

What creates the "Drama" is, instead of the victim and persecutor working through their differences, listening to one another's perspective and coming up with solutions to move forward, one (or both of them) complain to another person—the "rescuer"—about the other. The rescuer role is a caring third party who truly wants to be helpful and oftentimes will help at the expense of ignoring his or her own needs. Rescuers feel good about themselves by focusing on others rather than themselves.

When victims and/or persecutors go to the rescuer, the intent is often to get the rescuer on their side and "rescue" them. Instead of being open to taking responsibility for what they could do differently to improve the situation, or being accountable about how, unknowingly, they're making the situation worse, the victim and persecutor want the rescuer to validate why they are right and the other person is wrong.

At this point, at least two things might happen:

1. The rescuer offers advice or some type of solution and the tension between the victim and persecutor is temporarily defused. Yet the victim and persecutor, who really need to work through their differences, don't, and the conflict goes underground. The problem eventually re-emerges because it was never resolved.

2. The rescuer offers advice and if it doesn't work out, the tables are turned on the rescuer. The rescuer now becomes the victim. After an attempt to be helpful, the rescuer is blamed for the problem not being resolved because his or her solution didn't work. The victim is now persecuting the rescuer who tried to help.

No wonder this dynamic is called the Drama Triangle!

When Jerry went to his father to complain about how his stepfather wouldn't let him move into his brother's room, unknowingly, he was setting up a Drama Triangle with himself as a victim and his stepfather as the persecutor. The triangle didn't happen when Jerry turned to his father to rescue him because his father's response was, "Follow his rules, it's his and your mother's household." In other words, "This isn't your house and you have to respect your stepfather's decision." Jerry accepted the feedback from his father and moved back into his own room. Although Jerry didn't get what he wanted, he didn't stay a victim. He stayed in control of his emotions by taking responsibility for his behavior and de-escalated the conflict with his stepfather.

Learning the lesson of that first experience, Jerry deliberately prevented a Drama Triangle with each standstill he faced going forward.

Preventing Drama Triangles in the Workplace

Think about your workplace. Do you have "Drama Triangles"? When you have a disagreement with someone on your team, do you try to work it out with them or do you complain about the person to someone else, looking for validation of your position? If you do talk to a third party, are you looking for feedback on your blind spots and ways you can grow, or are you looking for someone to agree with you and blame the other?

How to Stay Out of Drama Triangles

Jerry's story teaches that the way to stay out of Drama Triangles is to take responsibility for your actions during conflict. Speak up, ask for what you want, and even when you don't get it, prevent conflict from escalating by staying in control of your response through your behavior.

Instead of focusing on hardships that could have easily hindered him reaching his full potential because of feeling like a "victim," he put in unrelenting effort, persevered through difficult experiences, and earned an education as a Master Chef. When he faced setbacks, he tapped into the skills he learned in high school through the SGORR program that equipped him to handle conflict and difficult conversations well.

In addition, Jerry astutely observed how his family members lived their lives and how they responded to financial challenges and racial bias. He listened and integrated their life stories to positively shape and catapult him "to carry myself well and to make sure I don't squander any opportunity." He used his positive family role models as inspiration to propel him forward when he faced challenges.

The driving force behind Jerry's pertinacity was believing in his self-worth. The resilience of his mom, grandmother, and aunt were, and continue to be, a source of strength to overcome challenges. His appreciation of being given opportunities that his father and uncle didn't have, due to racial bias, serve as inspiration, as Jerry said in his own words, "to represent where I came from well." All of this leverages Jerry's family strengths for lead a successful life, to be a successful leader, and to inspire his children to follow in his success.

References

The original Drama Triangle article: Karpman, Stephen. "Fairy tales and script drama analysis." *Transactional Analysis Bulletin*, 7(26), 39-43 (1968).

The comprehensive book on the Drama Triangle: Karpman, S. *A Game Free Life. The New Transactional Analysis of Intimacy, Openness, and Happiness.* San Francisco: Drama Triangle Publications, 2014.

Reynolds, David G. *Constructive Living.* Honolulu: University of Hawaii Press, 1984.

Self-Reflection Questions

1. In what ways has the Drama Triangle played out in your work environment?

2. Which of the three triangulation roles do you most relate to and in what way?

    a. Victim?

    b. Persecutor?

    c. Rescuer?

3. When you encounter a "standstill" during conflict, what did you learn from your family on how to respond?

4. In reference to David G. Reynolds' quote, "Feelings can be directly influenced by behavior," what behaviors are you willing to implement to be in more control of your response during conflict?

5. Conflict is an opportunity from which we can grow. What would it look like to not squander the opportunity that conflict brings and instead, listen to others' points of view to work through differences?

CONCLUSION

After I told a friend the title of my book—*How Did My Family Get In My Office?!*—her immediate response was "and how do I get them out?" Obviously my friend has a witty sense of humor.

The reality is, your family dynamics are in your office because you're there. You take you with you wherever you go, therefore your family will always be with you. Even if you were raised by foster parents, events from your upbringing and how people responded to those events, leave an imprint. Another friend said in response to my book title, "I lived in multiple foster homes growing up, that's why today I have a hard time trusting people. It's taken a conscious effort to let my guard down and trust employees because I couldn't trust anyone in my upbringing."

As you've been reading the leaders' stories, have you thought about the connection between how conflict was handled in your upbringing and how you handle conflict today at work—a.k.a. your Family Factor? Has there been a particular story that you related to? A scenario that took you back to your own family home?

In this closing chapter, I'd like to introduce you to The 4 Rs of Resolution, a powerful and memorable process to put your Family Factor to work for you. Throughout your career, you can revisit these 4 Rs and resolve to manage conflict effectively at work and grow in your own professional development.

The 4 Rs of Resolution: What You Can Do When Your Family Shows Up at Your Office

Because your family will always be with you, the answer isn't about getting your family out of your office. Actually, the answer is recognizing how your Family Factor shows up at work and making the conscious choice to develop the skills and strategies to respond productively. The 4 Rs of Resolution help you do just that in four complementary ways:

1. Regard the Scar – Acknowledge and address the emotional impact of events in your upbringing
2. Reframe to Stop Blame – Take control of your thinking about past events
3. Respect and Connect – Restore positive connections through boundaries
4. Resolve to Evolve – Be the author of your success

The 4 Rs are not a linear process. Like a circle that never ends, sometimes we need to revisit the 4 Rs to resolve conflict and restore relationships. The following section describes each of the 4 Rs of Resolution, including an example from one of the leaders you just met.

Regard the Scar

When you reflect on your family upbringing, "Regard the Scar," the first R of the 4 Rs of Resolution is recognizing how you were emotionally impacted by events in your upbringing. It's the acknowledgment of the strengths of your upbringing as well as the hurts, and your emotions associated with those hurts. While scars can be literal, such as from physical abuse, I'm referring more to the emotional scars from traumatic events.

You can't deal with what's not named. When you name it and work through the pain, you're taking the emotional charge out of the event, which ultimately leads to your changed behavior.

Such was the case in June's story from Chapter 3. Due to the chaos and conflict in her upbringing that was related to her dad's alcoholism, she acknowledged the emotional scars from living in unpredictability day to day. Later as an adult, she used alcohol to numb her feelings, until she chose recovery and addressed how the constant emotional chaos impacted her through sobriety, therapy, and involvement in Alcoholics Anonymous.

Like June, you may find it helpful to speak with a therapist, coach, spiritual advisor, or trusted friend who can help you work through any emotions associated with events from your upbringing. Many organizations offer Employee Assistance Programs (EAP), where you can confidentially speak with a licensed professional about issues in your personal life.

Regard the Scar Work Application: Be Aware of the Impact from Your Upbringing

The process of regarding your scars can take time. Avoid glossing over painful emotional scars and moving on too quickly. Practice pertinacity by taking your time and sorting through your emotions. In doing so, you're more likely to identify how similar patterns are showing up in your work setting today by how you interact with employees, co-workers . . . maybe even your boss.

Whether you grew up in an angry, tension-filled home or one with little conflict—either extreme doesn't provide healthy modeling on how to manage conflict effectively.

By addressing the emotional impact of events from your upbringing, you'll learn that you don't have to be scarred for life. You can heal the scars that are driving the negative ways of reacting to conflict and move on to a happy, bright future.

Reframe to Stop Blame

The second of the 4 Rs of Resolution is "Reframe to Stop Blame." After you recognize the impact of difficult events in your upbringing, take control of your mindset by reframing how you view the situation.

The purpose of reframing is to help you move from living in the past to living your life fully in the present—by taking control of your thinking and refusing to be a victim. You stop blaming your parents, your upbringing, or the dog, and take full responsibility for your behavior and life.

Mike, from Chapter 4, reframed his emotional scars due to his father's anger. Through counseling, he came to understand his parents better and to appreciate that they did the best they could based on behaviors that were modeled to them. He has no ill feelings towards his parents, and considers his father "perhaps the finest model of officership I ever witnessed."

When you "Reframe to Stop Blame," consider what life was like when those who raised you, either your parents or foster parents, were growing up. Remember that they, too, had influences that shaped their parenting style. This isn't to excuse abuse or other horrific behavior, rather to understand looking at relationships in context of their relationships, life events, and circumstances outside of their control.

Also, remember the positive events from your upbringing. When you find yourself dwelling on the negative aspects of your past, redirect your thoughts to strengths and skills you received as you were growing up and create a new perspective to help you move forward with your life.

Reframe to Stop Blame Work Application: Stop Blame and Identify Lessons Learned

Blame is not an action; it's an excuse for inaction. It's a decision on your part that doesn't have to be that way.

At work, when projects don't go as planned, an employee misses a deadline, or a huge mistake is made that results in lost revenue, reframe what happened and stop blaming. Blame is one of the fastest ways to breed defensiveness and stifle innovation. If people fear being blamed when they admit mistakes, they'll be more likely to cover up problems.

Just like events from your upbringing, when you reframe difficulties or setbacks as lessons learned and ways to improve going forward, you're creating an environment where people feel safe to speak up about mistakes and challenge the status quo.

Respect and Connect

The third R of the 4 Rs of Resolution involves respecting your family members and staying connected in the relationship when possible with boundaries.

This R is tricky, especially if there has been abuse or other traumatic events in your upbringing that some family members may still be denying and not taking ownership of. The purpose of "Respect and Connect" is to respect your family's heritage while at the same time deciding on the degree of connection and involvement that's healthy for you.

For example, in Chapter 9, Grace decided to stay connected with her mother out of respect for her as Grace's mother. The way she stayed connected was through the boundaries that Grace set, and from which she would not be moved—even when it entailed telling her mother, "I'm not willing to engage around this."

The opposite of "Respect and Connect" is having an emotional cutoff from your family by being emotionally distant from family or not seeing them at all. I often hear people say, "I have nothing to do with my family and it doesn't bother me at all"—when in reality they have difficulties in their work and home relationships, are highly reactive during conflict, and/or are codependent in how they function. These types of responses are red flags that emotional scars haven't been regarded and dealt with, which leaves unresolved hurts under the surface.

Even if you think you are emotionally disconnected from the roots of your family, if you tend to have non-productive, highly charged reactions during conflict, it's likely you're still connected more than you realize. "Respect and Connect" doesn't necessarily mean you maintain a close relationship with family. It does mean working through the conflicting feelings you have about emotional scars that haven't been healed.

Respect and Connect Work Application: Stay Grounded No Matter How Others Respond at Work

Perhaps you have a co-worker or boss who you've tried to get along with, and nothing seems to help. You've shown them respect and regardless of your attempts, you continue to get the cold shoulder or overlooked for a promotion. Or maybe you have employees who continue to exhibit poor performance or disruptive behavior, despite your attempts to help them improve.

Even when others don't respond to your efforts, extending respect and a hand towards connection is sometimes all you can do. Regardless of how others respond, your responsibility is to do your part to interact, without reacting negatively—especially when others don't respond in kind. Sometimes it means listening to another's perspective even if you don't agree, and letting go of having the last word. Other times, it means finding a common ground. At all times, "Respect and Connect" is treating everyone with dignity regardless of their behavior, ethnicity, religion, sexual orientation, background, values, or appearance.

Resolve to Evolve

The last R of the 4 Rs of Resolution is "Resolve to Evolve." It's your inner conviction that, regardless of events from your upbringing and emotional scars, you're determined to grow taking life lessons with you.

To "evolve" isn't a destination where you ever fully arrive. We're all constantly changing, hopefully in a positive direction. The intent of "Resolve to Evolve" is to consistently make the effort to develop and persevere . . . to move forward.

It's also having an inner peace about coming to terms with family events without lingering bitterness. It's a calm acceptance that even if differences aren't patched up, you're at peace.

Jerry from Chapter 11 showed us his "Resolve to Evolve" in that, regardless of facing several "standstill" situations when conflicts couldn't be resolved, he persevered. His "Resolve to Evolve" led him to achieve his goal of becoming a classically trained executive chef, part-owner of a restaurant, and a driving force in helping his employees thrive.

Resolve to Evolve Work Application: You Are the Author of Your Success

Having a "Resolve to Evolve" is an inner conviction that no matter what comes your way at work, you're willing to take responsibility as the author of your success. It's being willing to be vulnerable and allowing people to see your humanity. It's being receptive to feedback and recognizing shortcomings that are blind spots to you, yet are obvious to others. It's the willingness to be held accountable for making improvements.

Examples of "Resolve to Evolve" include:

- admitting when you're wrong
- asking for help
- showing curiosity and asking questions instead of assuming you have all the answers
- embracing change and showing flexibility
- allowing yourself to be uncomfortable and demonstrating humility by saying "I don't know"

"Resolve to Evolve" is the recognition that whether you are a leader or an employee, your behavior affects your entire work culture. Like all the leaders throughout this book, having a "Resolve to Evolve" means being committed to your personal and professional growth, which will enable you to succeed throughout your career and overall life.

Where to Go from Here

In addition to the Productive Conflict Management Strategies at the end of each of the leader chapters, apply the 4 Rs of Resolution to improve how you manage conflict. By taking action, you're making an investment in your own growth that will pay dividends in both your personal and professional success. The 4Rs of Resolution require honesty, humility, and the willingness to feel uncomfortable emotions. Surround yourself with people who will walk through the 4 Rs with you . . . without passing you a Kleenex!

Know that your pathway to addressing your Family Factor will be as unique as each of the leaders' stories in this book. There is no "right" way. Each leader found different ways to handle conflict productively—and with pertinacity, you will too.

Put Your Family Factor Into Action

1. **Regard the Scar**
   - Acknowledge how events from your upbringing are still impacting you—on and off the job.
   - Take the emotional charge out of past events, so you stay calm during conflict.

2. **Reframe to Stop Blame**
   - Take control of your thinking.
   - Focus on lessons learned as ways to improve going forward, not finding fault.

3. **Respect and Connect**
   - Mend relationships when possible and stay connected with boundaries.
   - Interact instead of react when differences arise.

4. **Resolve to Evolve**
   - Regardless of events from your upbringing, resolve to be your best self.
   - Be the author of your success, no matter what comes your way.

By taking action to address your Family Factor, you'll navigate through conflict with more ease. Making an investment in your own growth will pay dividends in both your personal and professional success.

"All of us have special ones who loved us into being."

—Mister (Fred) Rogers

ACKNOWLEDGMENTS

I have many special ones who loved this book into being and I'm so grateful for their love, encouragement, and support.

The first ones I want to acknowledge are my first leaders, my parents. Thank you for the foundation of love you provided and the values of integrity, character, and wisdom that you modeled. And to my sister, I cherish our conversations and appreciate your support.

I'm also grateful to each of the leaders in this book. Your willingness to share heartfelt stories about your family upbringing, in order to help others handle conflict better, is a reflection of your character, courage, and strength. It is an honor to know each of you.

Special thanks to my editor, Chris Murray. Your keen insights enhanced the relevancy and application of how family upbringing impacts all aspects of our lives, including at work. Thank you for your skill at distilling my "therapist speak" to everyday language while making the connection to each leader's Family Factor. Your intuition for the chapter layout and for the leaders to share their own stories and productive conflict management strategies was spot on. I'm especially grateful for your belief in this project from the beginning.

To Sam Horn, CEO of the Intrigue Agency, and my business and writing coach: Your words of encouragement that "corporate America needs my message" kept me going during re-writes. It is a highlight of my career to work with you. I'm in awe of your giftedness to bring words to life and intrigue to the ordinary.

To the Telemachus publishing team, especially to Johnny B. for your patience until we got the final product of the cover design, thank you for your creativity. Writing a book is one of the hardest things I've ever done and your guidance through the process has been greatly appreciated.

To friends and colleagues, Tony Pacione, Phyllis Hartman, Lauren Ostrowski, Patty Zacharias, Jim Fiesta, Sister Carole Riley, Brigitte Huffman, Wendy Gady, and Amy Noll, who were early readers: Thank you for your honest feedback about what content was helpful and what needed to go. Special thank you to Camille Sciullo, who helped bring clarity to the message of how our family shows up at work. Your wonderful sense of humor and straight talk brought a smile to my face even when it meant going back to the drawing board! Finally, to Becky Fox and Marilyn Howard, for your attention to detail in proofreading the final manuscript. I appreciate your time and diligence in catching extra spaces and punctuation mistakes.

To my speaker friends and colleagues of the Pittsburgh chapter of the National Speakers Association (NSA), I'm grateful to be part of a community that encourages each of us to serve our clients in the spirit of NSA founder, Cavett Robert: Mj Callaway, Bob Pacanovsky, Eric Kulikowski, Lynda Stucky, Carolyn Maue, Joe Mull, Jody Bechtold, Julie Ann Sullivan, Sarah Kohl, Laurie Guest, and Jolene Brown. Whether we were in a mastermind group together or we had a conversation to brainstorm an idea, your influence has helped me grow. Thank you.

To Renee Thompson, it's an honor to work alongside you to eradicate bullying and incivility in healthcare. Thank you for your support of this book and my work.

To Dr. E. Maurlea Babb, thank you for helping me understand my Family Factor. At times your words of wisdom "scratched like a kitten" and I knew you had just offered me "an opportunity for growth." I didn't always know at the time the lesson you wanted me to learn, and months (sometimes years) later I would finally "get" what you were saying. I'm grateful for your wisdom that I continue to apply in my life and work today.

To my fellow group members at Chrysallis, where together we shared struggles, laughter, and victories, I learned something from each and every one of you. I'm forever grateful for our time together that has left a lasting imprint on my heart.

To my therapy, coaching, and consulting clients and those who've participated in my workshops and keynote speeches, my deepest gratitude for the privilege of working with you. I admire your willingness to put in the hard work to make conscious choices and change patterns in yourself and your workplace when it would be easier to stick with the status quo.

Last, and certainly not least, I am grateful to my husband, Mark Fox. The first dance at our wedding says it all, "I could not ask for more." Your integrity, your generosity of spirit, your fun light-heartedness, and perspective enrich my life in ways I can hardly express. I love you.

Pablo Picasso said, "The meaning of life is to find your gift. The purpose of life is to give it away."

Humbly submitted, my gift is helping people create healthy relationships in their families and at work. I'm grateful to all the people above for contributing to this book, and if it helps you create the quality of life and relationships of your dreams, then my gift will have served its purpose.

ABOUT THE AUTHOR

Bonnie Artman Fox believes that magic happens when people have the courage to talk honestly about what is really going on in the workplace.

A Workplace Conflict Expert Bonnie is an accredited leadership coach, author, and professional speaker. She works with executive leaders and team managers who want to stop divisive behaviors, resolve conflict, and build the team trust needed to create a healthy work culture. Additionally, she is a content expert and leadership coach on conflict resolution and emotional intelligence for the Healthy Workforce Institute (HWI). In this work, Bonnie furthers HWI's mission to eradicate bullying and incivility in healthcare.

Having spent 25+ years as a psychiatric nurse and licensed marriage and family therapist, Bonnie has helped thousands of people resolve conflict in both their personal and professional lives. She specializes in uncovering the real roots of issues that undermine employees' performance, productivity, and team cohesiveness—an approach she's known for: The Workplace Family Factor™.

A sought-after speaker, Bonnie is a chapter leader in the National Speakers Association (NSA), serving as the 2020-2022 co-president of NSA Pittsburgh. When she's not working with companies and individuals, you can find her exploring this wonderful world of ours with her husband, Mark, and enjoying her role as Oma to her two fun grandchildren, Calvin and Theodore.

Free Resources for You and Your Workplace

If you're ready to take action on improving your team and workplace—I've got some great free resources just for you!

By investing in this book, you've gained access to an exclusive hub of resources to help you successfully navigate conflict when your family dynamics show up at work.

To claim access to your free resources, visit:
Bonnieartmanfox.com/familyfactorbook

To access the reader-only area of the resource library, please note you'll need this access code:

pertinacity

Grab a Complimentary Consult with Bonnie

If at this point you are wondering how to get help navigating conflict in your workplace—I'd love to connect with you.

As a reader, you're invited to schedule a complimentary consultation with me.

Hop on my calendar right now at:

bonnieartmanfox.com/consult

Here are a few of the ways I might be able to help . . .

Workplace Conflict Coaching

Coaching for individuals and organizations who want to stop divisive behaviors that tear teams apart and build trust and accountability.

Leadership Turnaround Coaching

Specialized coaching to help high performing leaders replace incivility, bullying, and angry outbursts with behaviors that create team cohesiveness.

Speaking and Training for Your Organization

Are you looking for a customized program for your next company conference or association meeting? I offer a variety of trainings, retreats, and inspirational keynotes on how to resolve conflict and create a healthy work culture. For current availability, please reach me at: bonnie@bonnieartmanfox.com

Made in the USA
Monee, IL
17 November 2020